THE ESS … OLD,
ANTIQU … IETAL

David Villanueva

Published by True Treasure Books
www.truetreasurebooks.net

ISBN: 978-0-9550325-4-7

Contents

INTRODUCTION

Since recreational metal detecting began some 40 years ago, a vast quantity of interesting artefacts have been uncovered. Old or even ancient cutlery are fairly frequent finds by metal detectorists, so it came as no surprise that Simon, a friend of mine, found a complete old base metal spoon on a beach with his metal detector. The real surprise was that we struggled to find any information to identify it and clearly others had met the same problem for I spotted an old base metal spoon, wrongly identified at an exhibition.

Around a hundred years ago, C J Jackson wrote *The Spoon and its history,* a paper covering mainly silver spoons from ancient times until the nineteenth century and F G Hilton Price wrote *Old Base Metal Spoons,* covering base metal spoons between the 14th and 18th centuries. Although there have been a number of books covering eighteenth and nineteenth century spoons since, there seems to have been very little coverage of earlier spoons. This is understandable to some extent as earlier spoons are not readily available to most collectors. The silver varieties are scarce and command very high prices, while almost all the base metal varieties have been lost or melted down and generally the only examples around have been excavated.

Nevertheless, I thought it would be worthwhile to produce this illustrated guide to spoons for finders, collectors, family historians and anyone interested in spoons from earliest times to the nineteenth century. I have basically divided the book into three sections: the first covers the development of spoons, particularly silver, from earliest times; the second covers old base metal spoons and the third, some continental spoons, many of which have been found in Britain. I sincerely hope that whatever old spoon you may come across or want information on, you will find it in this book.

THE DEVELOPMENT OF THE SPOON

Undoubtedly the spoon, which is now indispensable in our everyday life, has descended from very ancient times. Certainly as soon as the habit of eating pottage had been acquired, in a manner we would call civilised, there must have been spoons of some kind in use.

The earliest spoons were probably natural objects, the shells of aquatic animals such as the mussel, scallop, oyster and limpet, being the most readily obtainable natural spoons. The horns of various animals were doubtless also made into spoons as well as drinking vessels in the mists of time and when edge-tools came into use spoons, in all probability, were carved out of wood, bone and ivory.

Spoons of gold are specifically mentioned in the Bible and presumably, despite the lack of direct evidence, metals less precious than gold were also used for making spoons at least as early as the time of Moses.

The form and material of the spoons of the ancient Egyptians appear to have differed very considerably. There are examples in the British Museum of Egyptian spoons of flint, of wood and of ivory. The styles of many of these show the symbolism, which prevailed among those ancient peoples. There is one of slate (fig. 1) and two others of carved wood (figs. 2, 8) made in the form of the ankh or *crux ansata* (cross with handle), the symbol of Isis and life. The bowl of fig. 8 is very similar in form to that of several early Christian spoons and is not unlike the bowl of British spoons from the fourteenth to the seventeenth century.

A very peculiar spoon of carved ivory (fig. 3) has a shallow circular bowl and a very short handle shaped as the head of Athor or Isis, in her universal mother character typified by the cow, the ears of a cow being attached to the head of a woman. On each side of the head is carved an inflated asp.

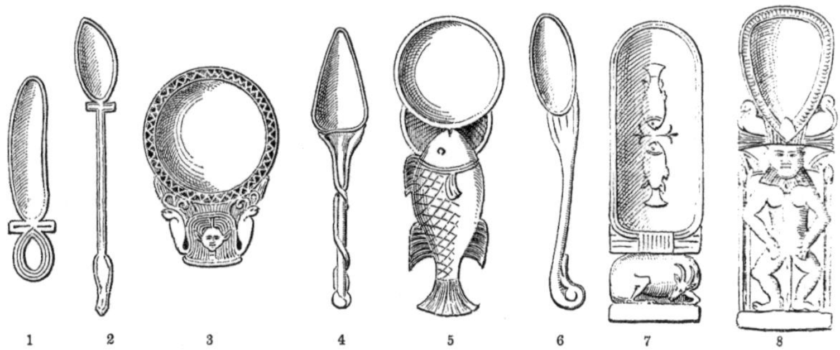

Figs. 1-8 Ancient Egyptian Spoons
Approx. 20% actual size

Purer symbolism appears illustrated in a wooden spoon from Thebes, carved in the shape of a lotus bud (fig. 4) symbolic of the productive power of the waters. In another wooden spoon, carved in the shape of a fish (fig. 5) the same productive power is symbolised. In this spoon the bowl is circular, the fish, which is carved on the face of the handle, being moveable and disclosing, when slipped on one side, a box or cavity sunk in the lower part of the handle. Another spoon (fig. 7) has two fishes head to head engraved in the bowl; the handle being carved in the form of a ram, symbolic of fertility and sexual freedom.

The spoons of the ancient Greeks and Romans were generally made either of bronze or silver. Forms vary considerably; some having very long pointed stems, while the stems of others are quite short and made into a variety of designs.

Some of the Greek bronze spoons are formed merely of hollowed circular discs with spikes attached to the back for handles; Roman bone spoons of this form are also very common. Others, with spiked stems, have bowls shaped like mussel shells, while many have bowls shaped like mandolins, with stems of various shapes. One of the latter (fig. 9) has a dolphin twisted round the lower part of the stem.

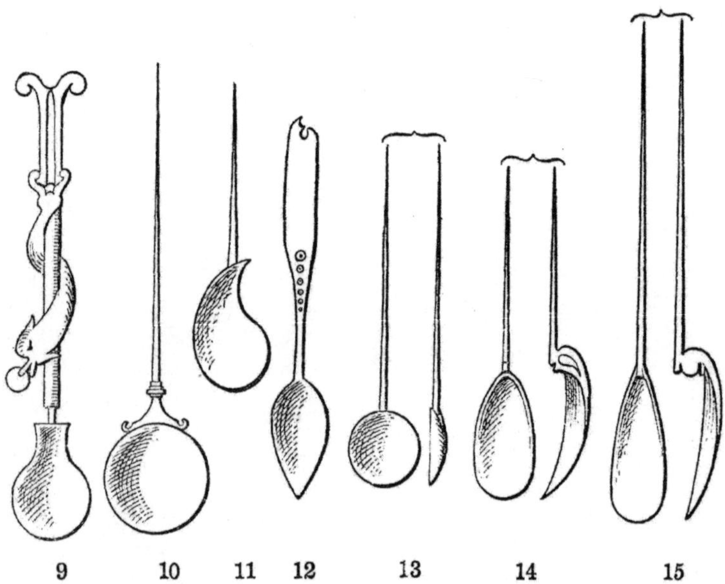

9 10 11 12 13 14 15

Figs. 9-15 Ancient Greek Bronze Spoons
Approx. 40% actual size

In the greater number of Greek and Roman spoons, as well as in the Early Christian (4th-6th century) spoons the predominate feature appears to be the union of the stem with the bowl. Beneath the bowl and supporting it for about half its length is a rectangular keel, which tapers away to nothing under the centre of the bowl, but increases in depth towards the stem, under which it curls up into a disc of about half an inch (1.3cm) in diameter. On the edge of this disc the stem is set, so that when the spoon is held in a horizontal position the bowl is about half an inch (1.3cm) below the stem. There are many modifications of this "keel and disc" form. In some, the keel is perforated, while in others the disc is curled like a spiral under the stem (see figs. 14, 15, 16, 18). The stems of these spoons are mainly plain spikes of various lengths. These spikes were used for opening shell-fish and extracting the edible part. They appear also to have been used in the eating of eggs, for Pliny, the first century Roman writer, states that the shells were broken or perforated with the spoons when eggs were eaten, to avoid evil consequences.

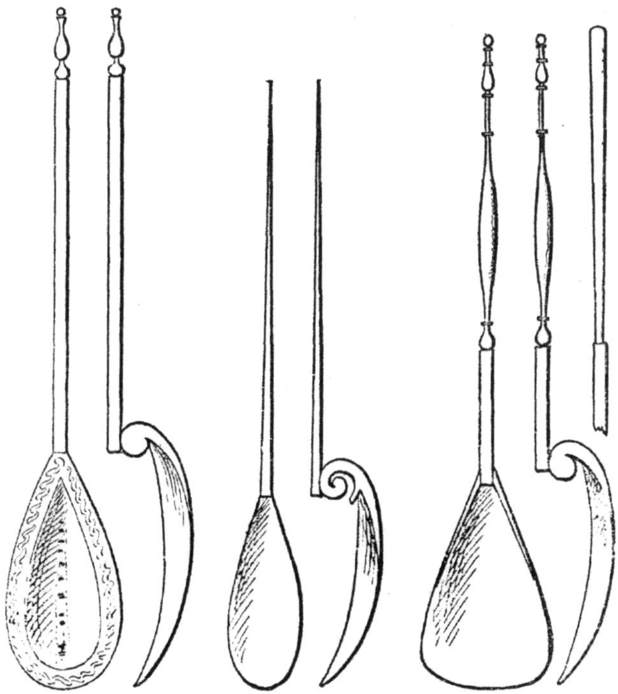

16 17 18

Figs. 16-18 Early Christian Silver Spoons
Approx. 40% actual size

Fig. 19 Etruscan Spoon of Carved Bone Length 5.2in/13cm

An Etruscan spoon of carved bone, found in the Isis tomb at Vulci (fig. 19), interestingly resembles some Dutch spoons of the seventeenth and eighteenth centuries.

Figs. 20 and 21 represent two Early Roman spoons. One is of iron, the other of silver. Near the bowl the stems are notched, probably for the purpose of resting them on the edge of a dish. The bowls of both are alike and one has been engraved inside with the figure of Mercury holding a purse in one hand, the caduceus in the other and his winged head-gear lying near his feet. At the end of the bowl are the figures of a cock and a goat and in the space, between Mercury's head and the cock, is a tortoise. Fig. 23 shows a similar Roman silver spoon found in Watling Street, near Rose Lane, Canterbury, Kent.

Among the Greek spoons in the British Museum there are two of silver, which were found at Cyzicus (fig. 24). The stem is in the form of a goat's foot, very carefully and delicately made; the bowl is quite like that of the everyday modern spoon. At the back of the bowl, where it joins the stem, there is a three-pronged tongue or lobe, which, supports the bowl and gives extra strength at the place where it is most required. In the museum of Naples, there is a similar silver spoon, which was dug up at Pompeii; so it seems that the design of this spoon was common to both Italy and Greece.

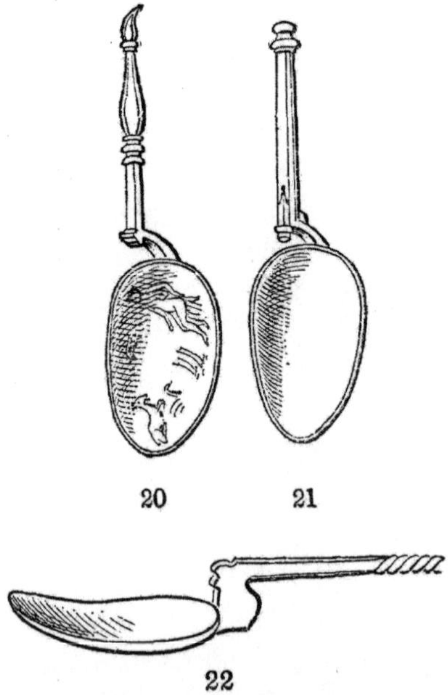

Figs. 20-22 Early Roman Spoons Approx. 40% actual size

Most of the Early Christian spoons in the British Museum are silver and many of them are very elegantly designed. Particularly noticeable are a pair (fig. 16), having the "keel and disc" features. The bowls of these are surrounded with a flattened rim, about a quarter of an inch (6mm) wide, on which is engraved between two lines a Vitruvian or classical scroll ornament which is continuous around the entire bowl. The stems are rectangular and uniform in thickness from the bowl to within an inch (2.5cm) of the end, where they terminate in baluster (short pillar) form, with a ball at the extremity. There is another pair (fig. 18) with the same characteristic "keel and disc" feature, the stems being in the form of turned balusters, from the handle end to within an inch and a half (3.8cm) of the bowl, where they are rectangular. The bowls of these bear a remarkable resemblance both in size and shape to the bowls of English spoons of the fifteenth and sixteenth centuries.

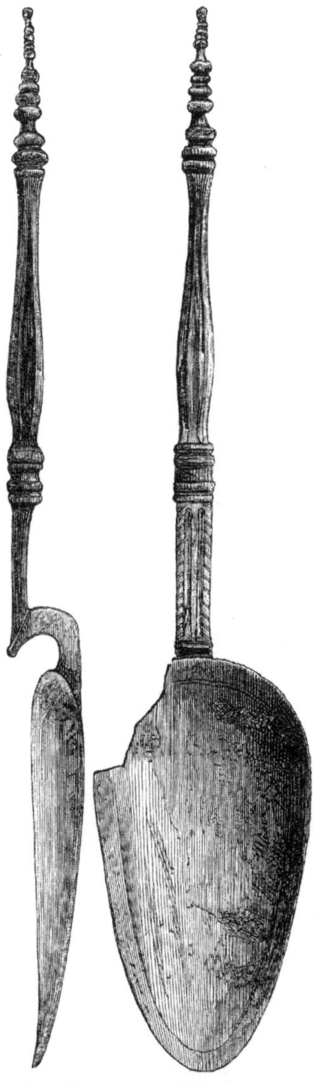

Fig. 23 Roman Silver Spoon
Length 6.7in/17cm

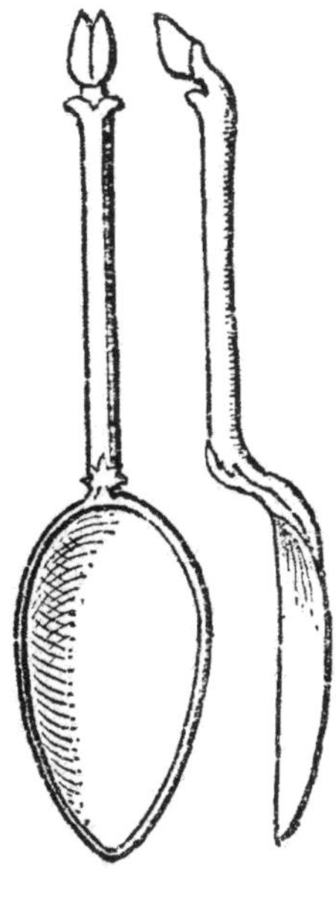

Fig. 24 Greek Silver Spoons
Approx. 20% actual size

An Early Christian spoon (fig. 25) in the British Museum bears a remarkable resemblance to the Victorian fiddle-pattern (fig. 71). It is silver, plain and small in size, being no larger than a modem teaspoon. It differs from the fiddle-pattern only in the shoulder next to the bowl being missing and the end of the stem being cut off square, instead of being rounded. But for this slight difference, it might very well be said that the Victorian fiddle-pattern spoon is a vulgarised copy of a relic of Early-Christian days. There is a Greek spoon of bronze (fig. 12) very similar in pattern although a little smaller. The bowl is narrower and more pointed and the stem is ornamented on its face with a series of small annulets, converging to a point in the centre of the slim part but the general resemblance of the two spoons is quite apparent.

Along with the spoons of the Early Christian period (4th–6th century) it may be convenient to refer to those curious bronze spoon-like objects of the Late Celtic period, a typical example of which is represented by fig. 30. Objects of the Late Celtic period probably date between 200BC and 100AD when Roman occupation in this country was firmly established. This date would account for the occasional discovery of such remains with or near Roman antiquities and also for the influence that their designs seem to have exercised over certain phases of Roman colonial art.

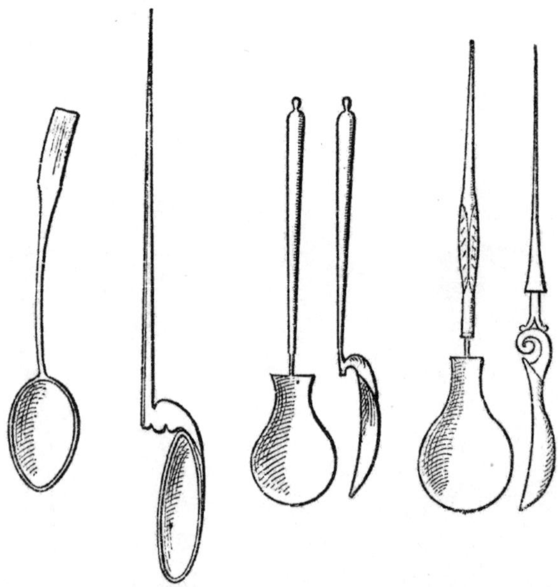

25 26 27 28 29

Figs. 25-29 Early Christian Silver Spoons
Approx. 40% actual size

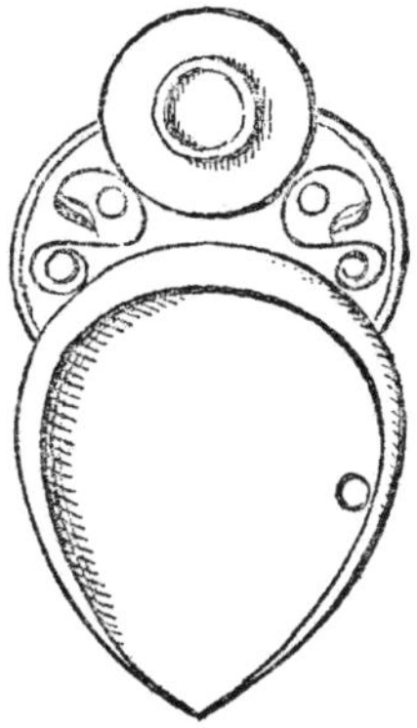

Fig. 30 Late Celtic Bronze Spoon from the Thames Length: 4in/10cm

These spoons almost always occur in pairs and are occasionally found at springs, wells or in rivers. One of the pair, always has a hole bored through it, invariably in the same spot, just below the lip and about mid-way on its left-hand side (looking from the handle towards the bowl). It is thought that these spoons were used for some form of 'baptism' ceremony where oil was drizzled through the holed spoon onto the 'baptised'.

In the dark ages, when the barbarians had crushed the power, luxury and refinement of the Romans; when our Saxon forefathers were gradually making this country their home in a life or death struggle, it could scarcely be expected that many would possess spoons of much value. There is, on the contrary, every reason to believe that during the first few centuries which succeeded the fall of Rome, the material of which the majority of these articles were formed was that which was most easily procured and could be shaped with little labour and workmanship.

The word " spoon" derived from the Anglo-Saxon *spon*, a chip, suggests wood as the material of which spoons of this period were commonly made and probably they were also made of horn and bone. There, however, is little evidence that metal spoons or at any rate those of precious metals, were in use to any appreciable extent during this period. For, although spoons of precious metal have been found in Anglo-Saxon graves, they have occurred but rarely and these have generally had small perforations in the bowl and cannot be ordinary domestic spoons. One such spoon (fig. 31), which was found at Chatham, is described as a silver spoon, ornamented with garnets; the bowl perforated and washed with gold, which is in some places much worn off. The garnets are encased in a projecting socket of silver. They are set on a gold foil embossed in chequers, to add lustre to the stone. On the edges of the handle is a delicate beading and in the interval of the setting are small circular marks. The reverse of the spoon has a neat brace fastened with six rivets, to mend a fracture near the handle, on the edge of which is impressed a chain of the above circular marks. The silver of the bowl is wafer thin. The suspension hole at the top with heavy wear at the back of the handle shows it to have been worn as a pendant. The handle and bowl have been hammered out of one piece of silver and the sockets of the stones are fastened with rivets, which penetrate the handle. It was found in a grave between the leg bones.

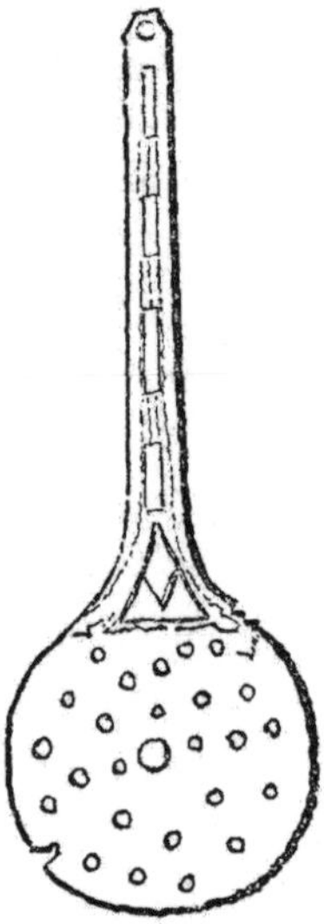

Fig. 31 Saxon Silver Spoon
Length: 5in/12.6cm

A somewhat similar perforated spoon but with five small holes only and a slighter handle, was found in an Anglo-Saxon barrow at Stodmarsh, Kent. At the junction of the bowl with the handle it is ornamented with a flat triangular-shaped garnet but otherwise the handle is plain.

A silver Saxon spoon was found together with some coins of Ethelwulf and Ethelstan at Sevington, North Wilts. Its total length is 8.5 inches (21.5cm). The bowl is only an inch (2.5cm) in width and somewhat fig-shaped. The long flat handle has a circular disc in the middle and at the end it is broadened out into an ellipse, being ornamented with an interlaced pattern over its entire length.

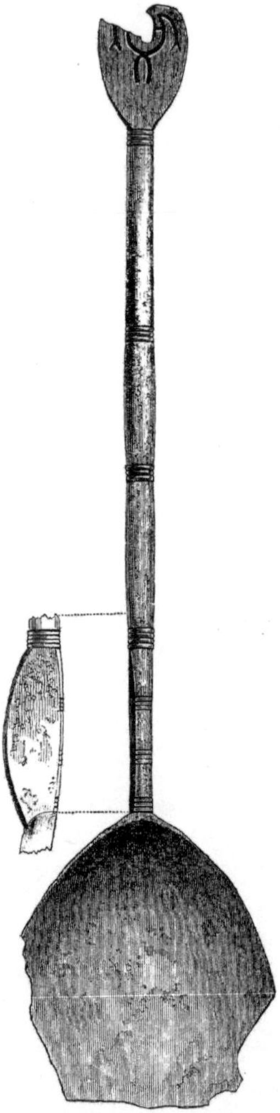

Fig.32 Early Spoon
Length: 6.1in/15.5cm

A spoon found at Desborough, Northamptonshire (fig. 32) appears somewhat Roman in style in that the lower part of the stem where it meets the bowl suggests a modification of the common Roman spoon without the classic ornamentation. The upper part of the stem, however, resembles the common form of baluster sometimes found in Anglo-Saxon work. Whether this spoon is late-Roman, Anglo-Saxon, or Norman Romanesque, is an interesting speculation. It measures 6.1 inches (15.5 cm) in length over all and is of base silver or white metal; both extremities are imperfect, having been broken off.

Of medieval spoons, one of the earliest and perhaps the most interesting example in existence is the coronation spoon preserved among the regalia in the Tower of London (fig. 32a).

It has most probably been used in the coronation of our monarchs since the twelfth century. Its style of ornament seems to prove that it was made at that period. It is of silver gilt, with four pearls in the broadest part of the handle. The bowl, which is thin, has an elegant arabesque pattern engraved on its surface. Unfortunately the enamel has been destroyed either accidentally or wilfully, but the rough surface between the filigree work proves its former existence. It is used to hold the oil for anointing the monarch at their coronation and a ridge divides the bowl down the middle, into two hollow parts. It is 10.25 inches (26cm) long and weighs 3.4 ounces (96.4 grams).

The domestic spoons in common use in the Middle Ages appear to have been made either of wood or horn, for while bone, ivory, serpentine, rock-crystal and glass were occasionally made into spoons and sometimes garnished with precious metal, these are only "fancy spoons" and certainly weren't in common use. Gold spoons, except in rare instances, seem to have been confined to the monarch's use and spoons of silver were to be found only in the homes of the wealthy.

Spoons of pewter, brass and tinned iron appear to have been very common from about the fifteenth century and probably earlier. There was also a type of brass called " latten" of which spoons and other domestic utensils were made.

Although various kinds of metal spoons were used in Britain from the thirteenth century, there is still abundant evidence to prove that wood and horn spoons were the kinds most commonly found in this country and Europe until the late sixteenth century. However, silver spoons accurately reflect the prevalent form at any time during the past 600 or 700 years, because, unlike gold, silver was not so scarce and valuable to prohibit its use but valuable enough to make silver articles very desirable and specifically referred to in wills and inventories. Their care and preservation has resulted in many excellent examples of antique silver spoons being found in collections throughout the country and the system of hall-marks since 1478, has enabled, the year to be fixed in which any fully marked specimen of gold or silver was assayed.

The earliest entry relating to English spoons appears to be that in the will of Martin de St. Cross, of the year 1259. It simply refers to a dozen silver spoons without any clue to their size, weight or shape but in later entries the weight and description is given in many instances enabling many of the spoons to be identified as resembling examples which have been handed down, through the centuries.

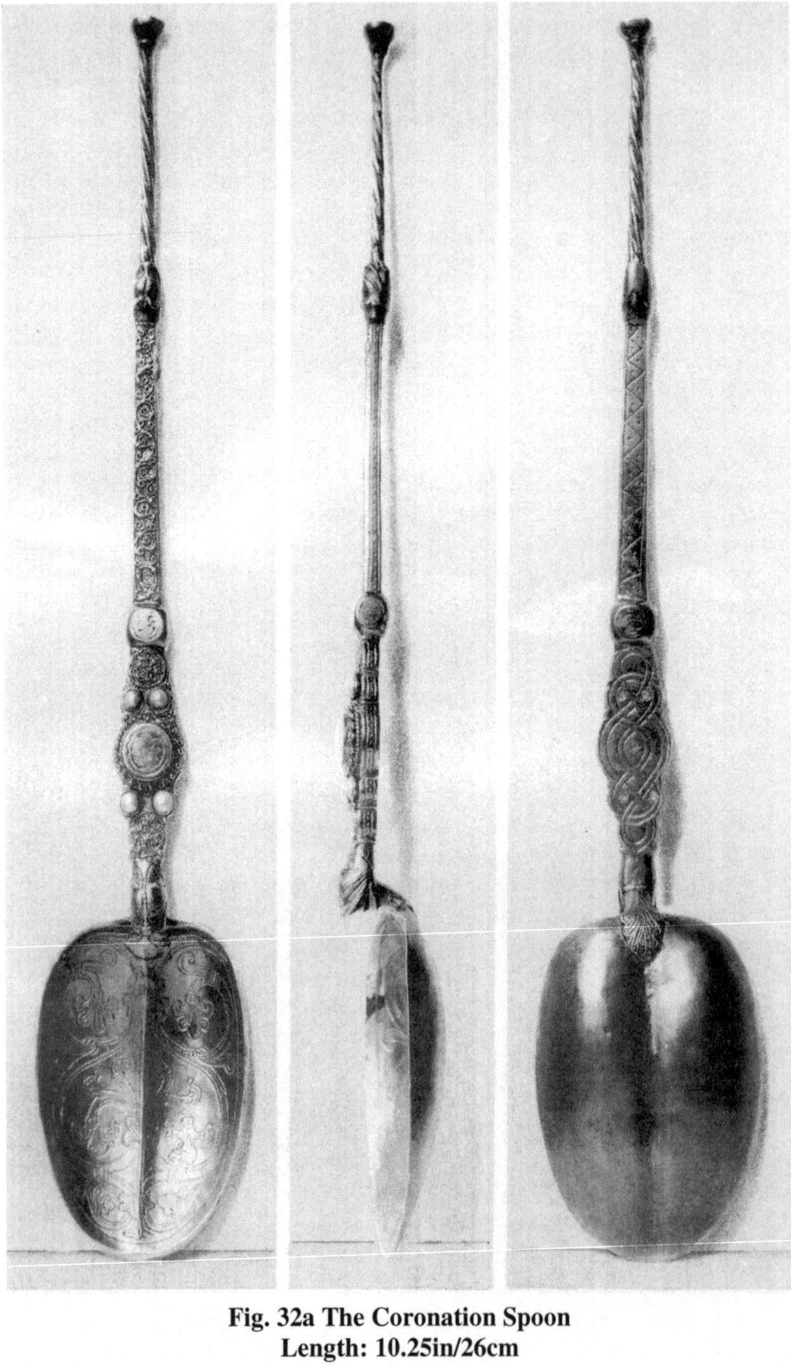

Fig. 32a The Coronation Spoon
Length: 10.25in/26cm

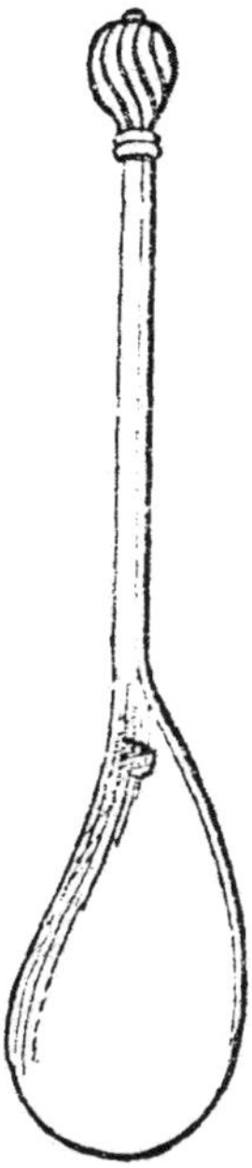

Fig. 33
Writhen Knop
1488-9
Length:
6.2in/15.6cm

An entry in the wardrobe accounts of Edward I in 1300 mentions seven gold and eight silver spoons marked in the stem with the mark of Paris (the fleur-de-lis), which shows they were brought from France.

An inventory of the crown jewels of Edward III taken in the year 1329 mentions "36 silver spoons plain white stamped with the leopard, value 59s. 10d." Another entry in the same inventory mentions five spoons of gold weighing 10s. 10d. (8.7 ounces or 247 grams), value £9. 12s. 6d. From these two entries together it is clear that the spoons of the time of Edward III weighed about an ounce and were much lighter and less bulky than most of those of the Tudor and Stuart periods.

Regardless of the English domestic spoon form before the fourteenth century, from then until about the mid-seventeenth century, it consisted of a fig-shaped bowl, curved upwards to an extent becoming incapable of holding a complete spoonful of liquid. The wider part of the bowl being at the base, and the narrower next the stem or "stele," which was commonly hexagonal or, in the language of the period, "six-squared," terminating in most cases with a knop. The shape of the knop varied greatly and consisted of acorns; square (or "six-squared knops"); hexagonal spear-heads or "dyamond poyntes"; strawberries, balls, or scallop shells; busts of the Blessed Virgin (sometimes called, "maidenheads"); birds of some kind, such as owls, falcons or columbines; mitres; the figure of an angel, saint or apostle; an ornamental knob or baluster (balusters with a flat end are known as "seal tops"). During the Tudor period a lion sitting holding a shield with its fore paws became popular and from the time of the Tudors until shortly after the Restoration, the stems were often cut off at the end in a diagonal line sloping outwards from the face, and so finished without a knop of any kind. Spoons with such stems were generally referred to as "slipped in the stalks."

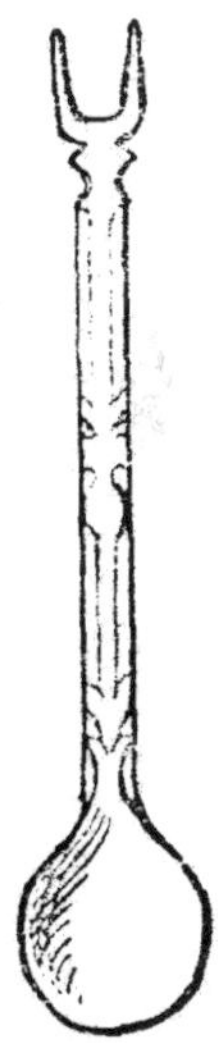

Fig. 34 Spoon and Fork Combined
Length: 4in/10cm

One of the earliest English domestic spoons known is a London-made silver spoon with fig-shaped bowl, "six-sided stele," and gilt "dyamond poynte" (fig. 35). Attributed to the fourteenth (or possibly early fifteenth) century, this spoon is much thinner in the stem and less bulky overall than of later spoons. The only mark it bears is an uncrowned leopard's head, stamped (chin upwards) in the bowl. The leopard's head is surrounded by a circle of raised dots, similar to the dotted circle on contemporary coins.

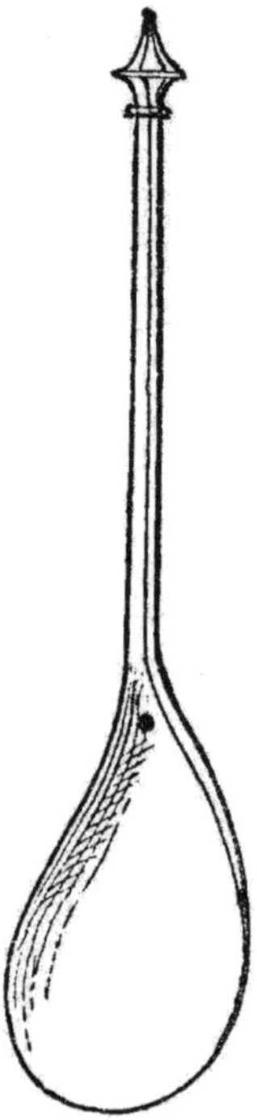

Fig. 35 14th Century Diamond Poynt Length: 6.4in/16.2cm

The Scarborough folding spoon (fig. 36) appears to have been made probably for persons travelling who carried their own spoons in their pockets. It is silver and terminates with a diamond point. Its date has been assigned to the fourteenth century. Making allowance for the short stem, the grotesque head, which slides over the joint and the more clumsy finish of the provincial workmanship the spoon generally closely resembles the "dyamond poynted" spoon just described.

Fig. 36 Silver Folding Spoon found at Scarborough Length: 5in/12.5cm

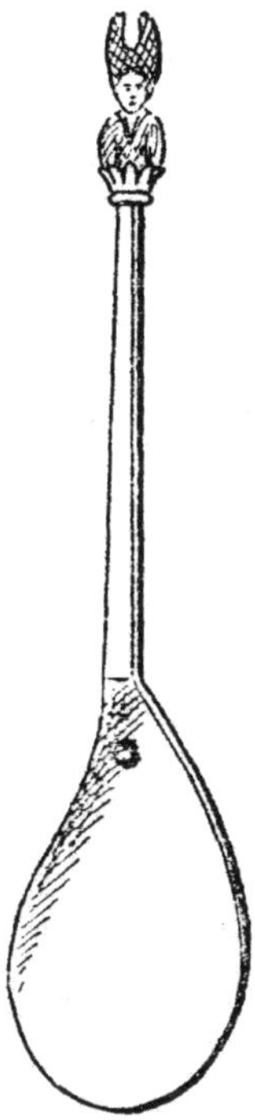

Fig. 37 15th Century Horned Head-dress Length: 6.7in/17cm

A base-metal spoon, knopped with the bust of a lady in a horned head-dress of the time of Henry V (fig. 37), is an interesting relic of the middle ages, which undoubtedly from the style of the head-dress, belongs to the first half of the fifteenth century. Interestingly also, it confirms the slender make of the spoons of this period, as compared with those of later date.

The acorn, which is the earliest form of knop that has been found described in any published document, was, it seems, much favoured during the fifteenth century, but not so much afterwards, in the acorn-knopped spoons of later date the acorn is larger.

Although the termination of the stem varied considerably, only a few forms appear to have been common, the most popular being the apostle termination. These spoons were often made in sets of thirteen, twelve being knopped with the apostles, each distinguished by his emblem, the knop on the thirteenth being an image of Christ, the left hand holding the orb and cross, the right hand raised in blessing. In the earliest apostle spoons the nimbus or halo is set at the back of the apostle's head (see fig. 38), while in those of later date it is a flat circular disc fixed on the top of the head (see fig. 39).

The "seal top" appears to have occupied the second place in popular favour, while of the other forms, "slipped in the stalk" seem to have been the most common.

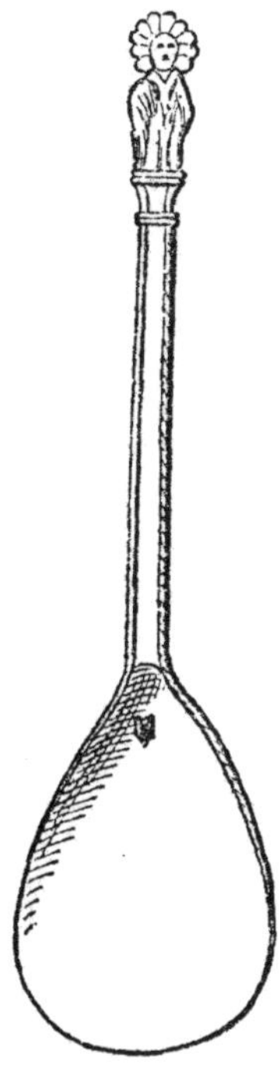

Fig. 38 Early Apostle Spoon Length: 7.2in/18.3cm

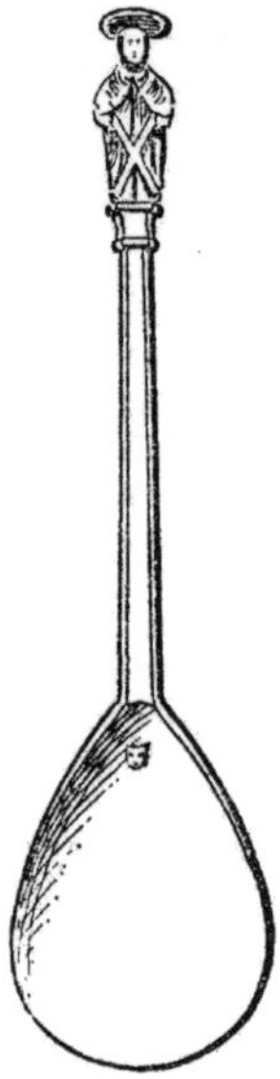

Fig. 39 Later Apostle Spoon
Length: 7in/18cm

In the case of nearly every genuine "knopped" silver spoon, a careful examination will show that the stem and bowl have been hammered out of one piece of metal, and that the knop has been cast and secured to the stem by a soldered joint, usually a "V-joint." A V-shaped notch having been cut out of the top of the stem and a small piece of cast metal attached to the knop, shaped to fit into this notch, the two parts are joined so that the bottom of the knop moulding rests on the edges of the V notch, the joint being strengthened by the two prongs gripping the cast burr of the knop, which fits into them. There may be genuine examples with their knops attached in a different manner but they are rarely found.

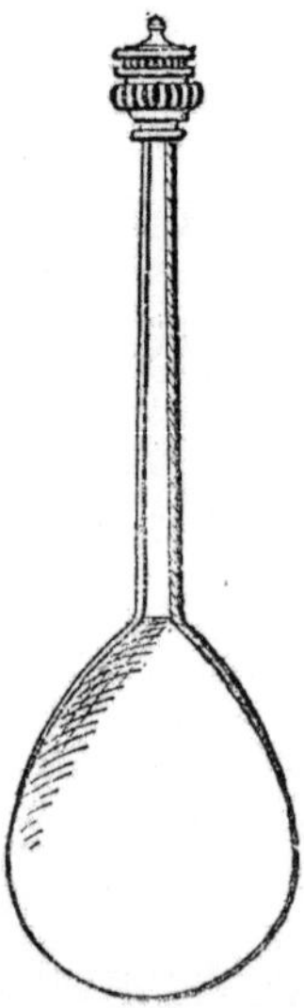

Fig. 40 Baluster Knop
Length: 6in/15cm

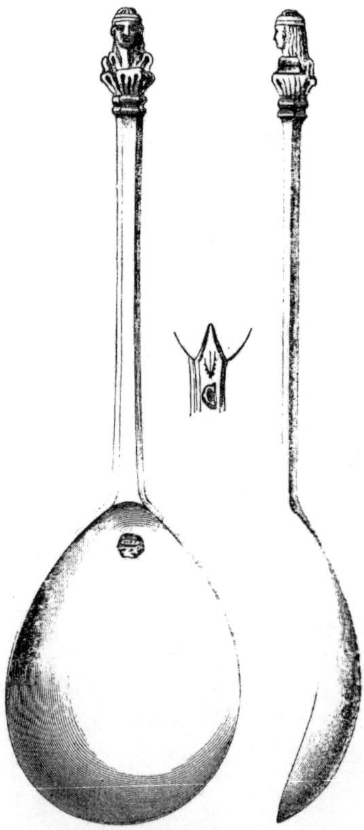

Fig. 41 Maidenhead Spoon, London 1520-1
Length: 7in/17.7cm

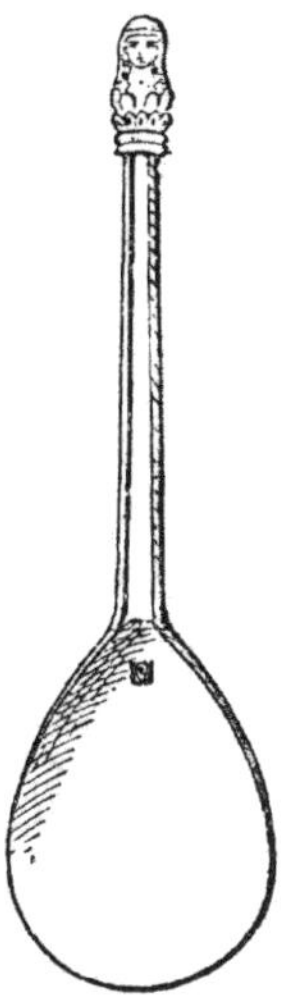

Fig. 42 Maidenhead, London 1553-4 Length: 6.3in/16cm

Fig. 43 represents a London seal top spoon of the year 1560-1. It has a somewhat uncommon form of baluster, in that its lobes are larger than usual, and there is a rather long neck between the lobes and the torus moulding at the end of the shaft. Another spoon (fig. 44), of 1562-3, has a baluster under the seal top, somewhat like the latter but without the long neck. This is a typical sixteenth century seal top spoon. In large later seal top spoons the baluster is often more elaborate and occupies a greater length of stem than in sixteenth century examples.

Two English medieval spoons; one of silver knopped with a "maidenhead" (fig. 45), the other (fig. 46) of pewter with a strawberry knop., differ somewhat in form from the majority of the spoons of their respective types.

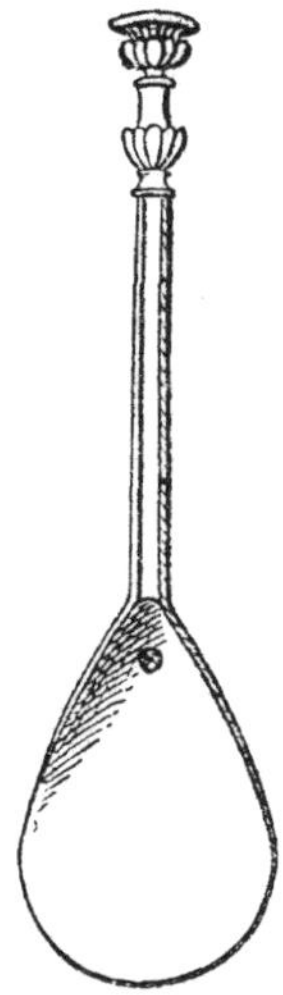

Fig. 43 Seal Top, London 1560-1 Length: 6.9in/17.4cm

Fig. 47 represents a spoon knopped with an acorn and the base metal spoon with ornamental stem knopped with a figure in a plumed hat (fig. 48) appears to be continental, probably French, of the time of Francis I (1515-47).

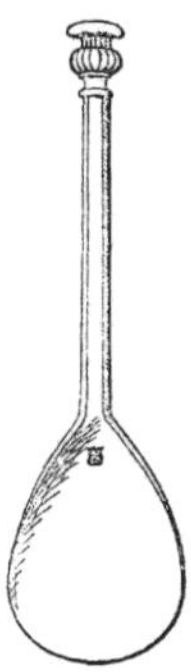

Fig. 44 Seal Top, London 1562-3 Length: 6.1in/15.6cm

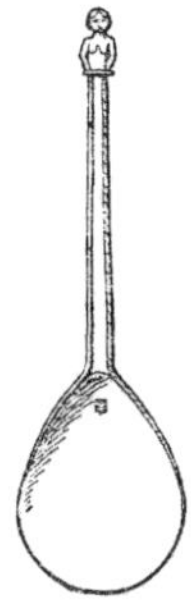

Fig. 45 Maidenhead Spoon Length: 5.7in/14.4cm

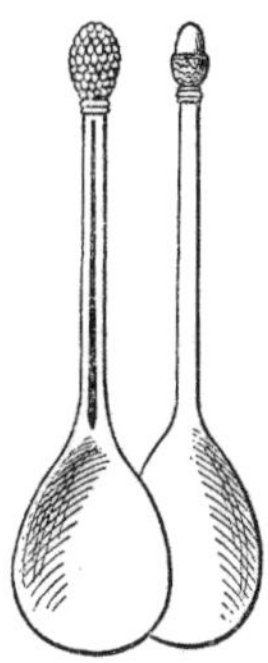

Fig. 46 Strawberry Knop, Pewter
Fig. 47 Acorn Knop Length: 6in/15.3cm

Fig. 48 Continental Base Metal Spoon Length: 5in/12.6cm

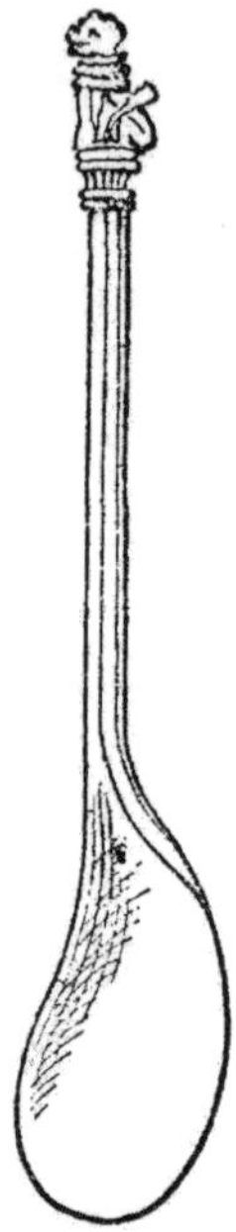

Fig. 49 Sitting Lion Knop, London 1592-3 Length: 6.8in/17.2cm

The silver spoon knopped with a lion sitting (fig. 49) has the London hall-marks for 1592-3. It is an interesting example of a type described in contemporary documents as a "silver spone with a lyon, holding a scutcheon at the end gilt;" a type which is found only from the time of Henry-VIII. to James I.

The spoon of silver "slipped in the stalk" (fig. 50) is of the year 1598-9. It is a good Eltzabethan specimen of this form of spoon, known from around 1500.

Fig. 51 represents a spoon like one "of silver-gilt, the stele six sided, with a scripture upon it, the knop being round and decorated with leaves, and the letters WT. and P. engraved at the end. This spoon, which is fully marked for the year 1610-1, is a fine specimen of the commonest seal top type, which was popular during the sixteenth century but is rarely found of later date. It is evidently a christening spoon, for the "scripture" on the stele, which reads "Margaret Austen born the 11 day of September 1610," corresponds with the date letter stamped on the back.

Fig. 52 represents a silver "master spoon," of the year 1637-8, such as that referred to in the 1554 inventory of Thurston Tyldesley, in the entry "13 sylver spones with the image of God apon one of them." At the extreme end of nearly every spoon knopped with either an apostle or a seal-top, there will be found a plate or flat piece of metal, either circular or hexagonal in outline; but the master spoon differs from others in that it has the figure of a dove, symbolic of the descent of the Holy Ghost upon God the Son, raised in low relief on the upper surface of this plate.

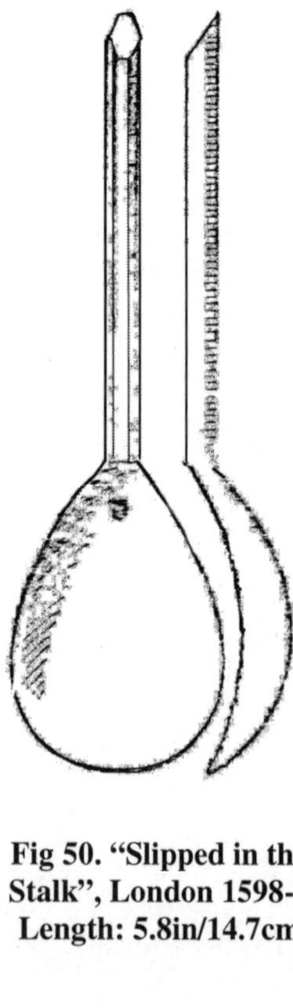

Fig 50. "Slipped in the Stalk", London 1598-9 Length: 5.8in/14.7cm

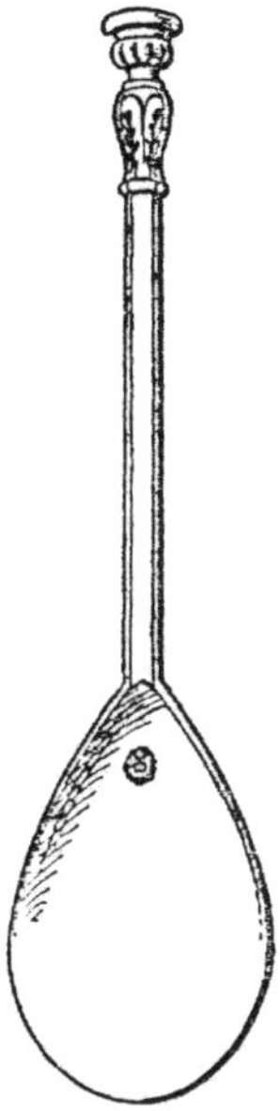

Fig. 51 Seal Top, London 1610-11 Length: 7.2in/18.3cm

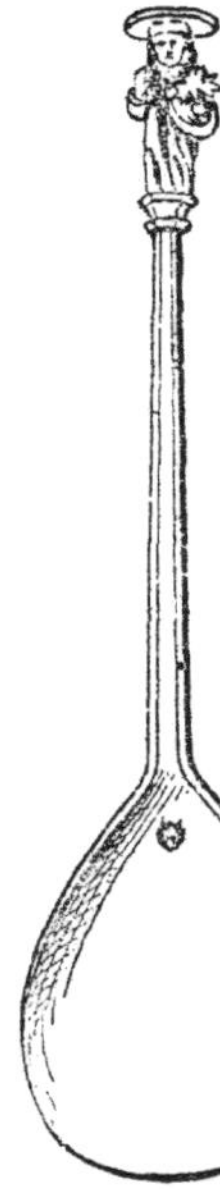

Fig. 52 "Master Spoon", London 1637-8 Length: 7.2in/18.3cm

Before leaving sixteenth century spoons, there is a brass spoon, which deserves mention, as it probably belongs to that period. Fig. 53 shows that the bowl is of the early type. The stem, however, is four-sided and moulded cross-wise like a square baluster. At the end of the stem is a long notch, in which it would appear, judging from the pin-hole near the extreme end, a wheel must have formerly revolved. It is probably a cook's spoon, the wheel being very likely for decorating pastry.

It is a remarkable feature that the shape of the bowl changes on spoons during the seventeenth century, from how it was in the early part and had been for at least two centuries previously, gradually becoming wider in proportion near the stem and narrower at the base. This change is very noticeable in two spoons. The first is an apostle spoon (fig. 54), from which the date letter has been worn away but which, from the maker's mark, **I · I**, in a plain shield, was probably made between 1640 and 1657, the outline of the bowl is very nearly a true ellipse. In the bowl of the second, a Puritan spoon (fig. 55) of the year 1662-3, there is not the least semblance left of the fig-shape. The wider part of the bowl is next to the stem, the narrower at the base, and generally its form approaches that which came into fashion soon after 1660. This gradual change in the shape of the bowl is noticeable in nearly every London-made spoon from about 1625-1660.

The only exception being spoons which appear to have been made to match earlier ones; although knopped spoons were not generally made after 1660, the Armourers' Company, had three seal top spoons dated 1687, 1690 and 1745.

Fig. 53 Brass Cook's Spoon Length: 6.5in/16.5cm

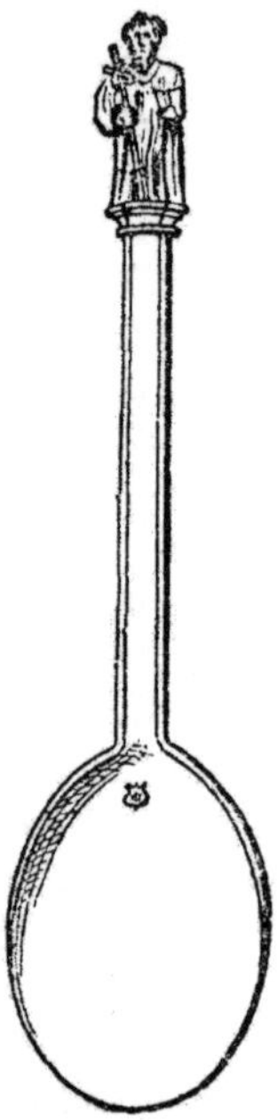

Fig. 54 Apostle Spoon with Later Bowl
Length: 7in/17.7cm

By 1670 the English spoon became completely changed, not only in the bowl but also the stem, which had been hexagonal and nearly as thick as wide, became quite flat, much wider and thinner, especially at the extreme end, curling slightly upwards and splitting into three parts. The lower part of the stem, which earlier was finished off in a short angle at the top of the bowl, now continued to form of a tongue or "rat's tail" over half way down the back of the bowl. But before the new form of spoon became established, many examples of the period show some features of the old form.

Whether the new form was introduced from the continent, or was developed in this country from the earlier "slipped in the stalk" spoon is open to conjecture. The view that the new fashion was imported is supported by the fact that the new form of bowl appeared earlier in continental spoons and that any ornamentation was decidedly continental. On the other hand, the "home-development" theorists argue that the hexagonal stem only needs progressively hammering thinner and ornamenting by inserting two slits and curling the ends upwards, as seen in the spoon of 1678-4 (fig. 56). The added tongue on the back of the bowl was not found on all spoons of the new form, as evidenced by an Exeter spoon dated 1676.

The theory of insular development having been considered it may be worthwhile to examine the form and ornamentation of a continental spoon (fig. 57). The tongue is made to form the centre of an acanthus leaf, which is chased on the bowl. Unfortunately it has no mark indicating its date, however it is undoubtedly seventeenth century work and its outline and ornamentation strongly suggest that it or a similar spoon, inspired the fabrication of some English spoons of the late seventeenth century.

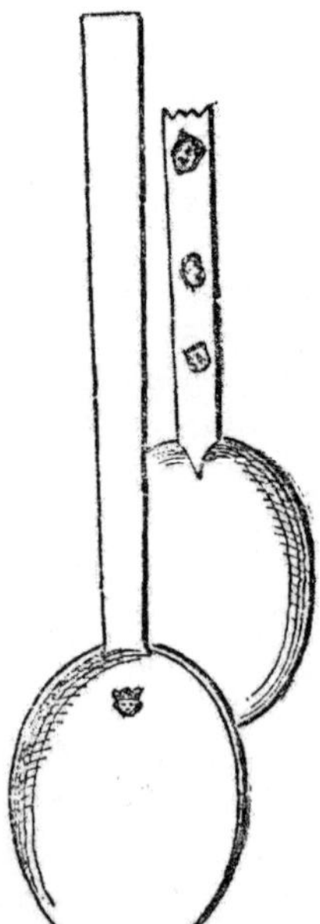

Fig. 55 Puritan Spoon, London 1662-3
Length: 7in/17.7cm

A Tyrolese spoon (fig. 58) has a substantial tongue under the bowl, constructed to keep the spoon flat on a table, even when filled with liquid. It has a massive stem curved sharply outwards from the tongue, which extends well beyond the bowl. The stem has a flat escutcheon terminal.

The tongues on the backs of English spoon bowls of the late seventeenth century vary considerably in pattern. In a child's spoon of 1670-1 the tongue is very raised, closely resembling the later rat-tail, while in two large spoons of 1674-5 and 1677-8 it is only slightly raised and is accentuated more by being hollowed on each side of a central ridge than by additional metal. There is no surface ornamentation on either of these spoons, but one of 1683-4 is ornamented with raised foliated work in low relief on the stem face and the back of the bowl. A spoon of 1692-3, similarly ornamented on the stem face, has no ornament on the back of the bowl, except the tongue, which, more elaborately than usual, is composed of a series of ribs with beads in the centre, decreasing in size as they approach the point of the tongue. A spoon of thirteen years later has a tongue almost identical in pattern.

Some Scandinavian spoons seem to fall midway between the medieval type and that of the third quarter of the seventeenth century. The most interesting specimens are shown in figs. 59, 60 and 61 and although difficult to date, they are probably seventeenth century. Those with little rings for attaching to a watch chain, were used for drinking strong liquors from a communal bowl, where every man brought his own spoon.

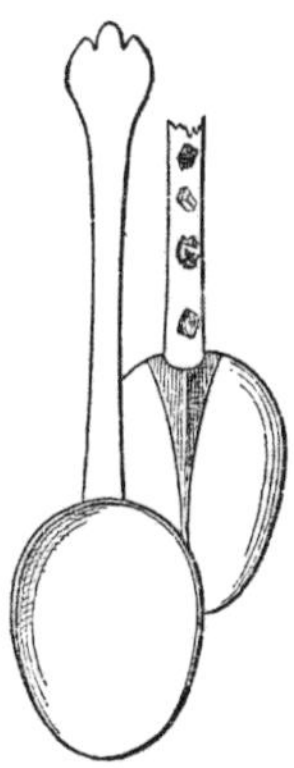

Fig. 56 Split End, London 1673-4 Length: 7in/17.7cm

Fig. 57 Foreign Spoon Length: 7.8in/19.8cm

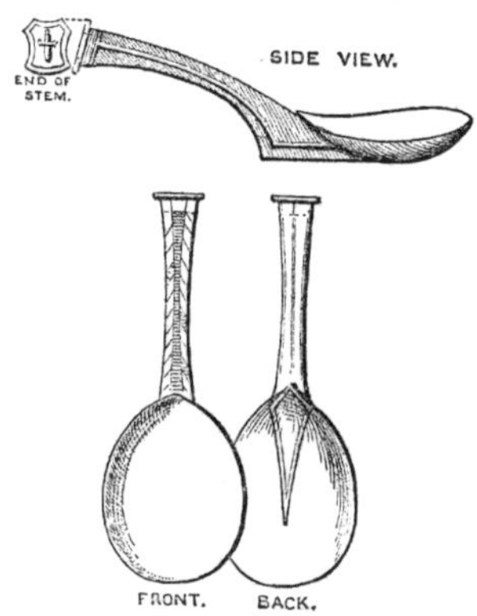

Fig. 58 Tyrolese Spoon Length: 4.7in/12cm

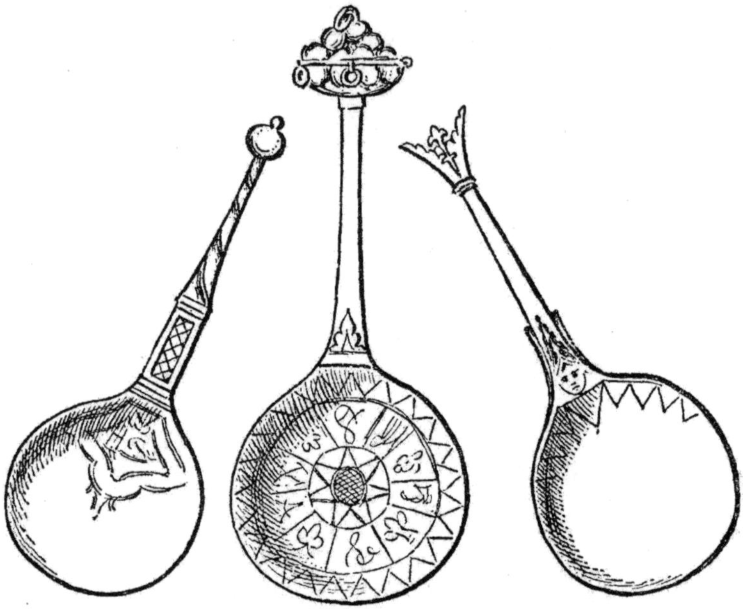

Figs. 59, 60, 61 17th Century Scandinavian Spoons
Approx. 50% actual size

A silver-gilt engraved spoon (fig. 62) of London make and stamped with the leopard's head and lion passant of the period 1678 - 1696 has not, nor ever had, either date-letter or maker's mark. But a similar spoon, made about the same time has the date-letter for 1689-90. The engraved work on both is rich and elegant but continental in character and more likely to have been suggested by French work of the Louis XIV period, than by any English work at that time.

During the last decade of the seventeenth century, the English spoon seems to have undergone an almost continuous change of form. A spoon of 1697-8 has the split end, similar to that of twenty years earlier, but the tongue is very like the ordinary rat-tail, which succeeded the more elaborate form. The stem of a 1699-1700 spoon (fig. 63) has no splits at the end, which is finished off in a waved line, with the centre part being turned slightly upwards; the back of the bowl has the common form of rat-tail which endured for about thirty years from this date. The bowl itself is narrower in proportion to its length, than in earlier spoons and this change appears to have been pretty general at the end of the seventeenth century. A spoon of 1706-7 is marked by another change, in that the stem, instead of being flat throughout its entire length, is rounded on the face for half the

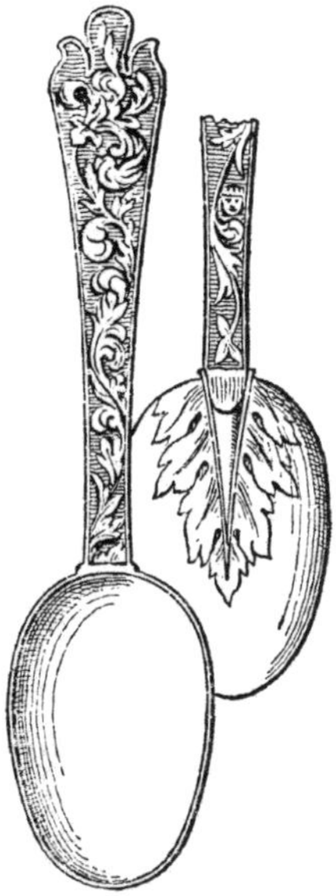

Fig. 62 Silver-Gilt Engraved Spoon c. 1690 Length: 8.3in/21cm

distance from the bowl upwards. This spoon and the wavy end may well be called "transitional," for they have features in some respects common to the spoons of the seventeenth and eighteenth centuries. In the later spoon, however, the only seventeenth century feature is the flatness of the stem in the upper half, while in the other, which is only a few years earlier, with the exception of the clefts, nearly every feature of the Charles II (1660-85) spoon is still preserved.

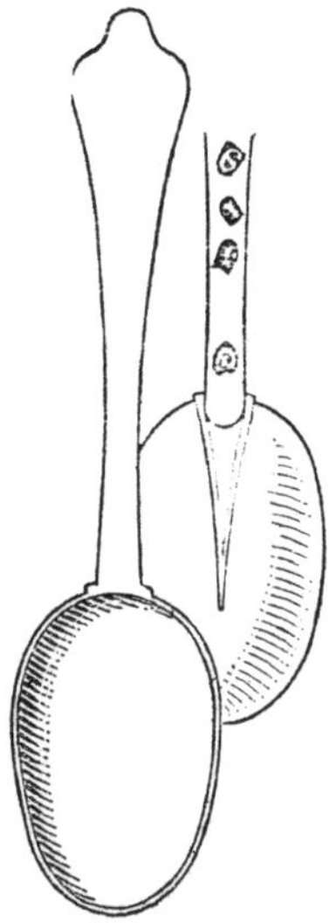

Fig. 63 Wavy End, London 1699-1700 Length: 8in/20.4cm

The next modification was made to the upper half of the stem (see fig. 64) where the flatness present for about 50 years disappeared. The waved line at the extreme end with its projection in the centre also disappeared and for the first time apparently, in English spoons, the outline of the end continued round from side to side in one unbroken curve. The centre part of the end of the stem was made thickest by hammering back the central projection to obtain the continuous curve, an assumption supported by a spoon (fig. 65) having this projecting part curled over without being united to the main body of the stem. The end was still turned upwards towards the face, where a sharp ridge was formed, which continued from the thick part at the end to about half way down the stem, where it faded away into the lower part, where the face was rounded. On each side of this ridge a depression was made sloping towards and, becoming quite thin at the edge. The upper half of the stem face appeared as two long narrow concave channels, divided by a sharp ridge curving upward at the end into a small raised plateau.

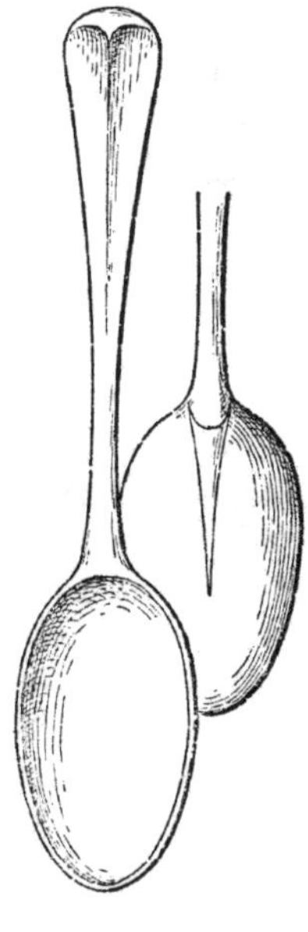

Fig. 64 Rounded End Length: 8.3in/21cm

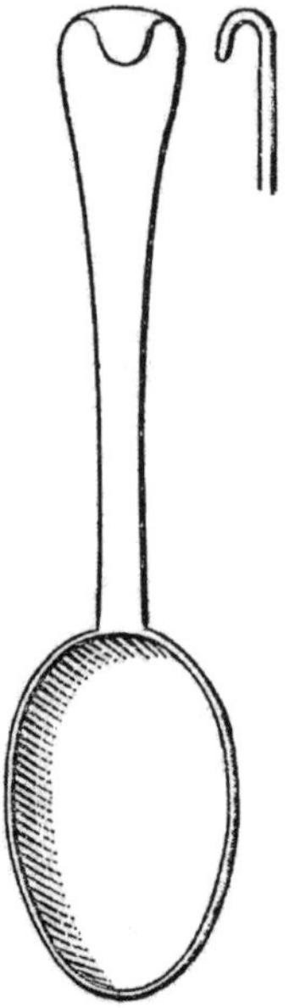

Fig. 65 Length: 7.8in/19.8cm

This rat-tailed spoon with the new ridged and channelled stem (fig. 64), made in England for about 25 years, appears to have been an English innovation rather than being introduced from Hanover. The new spoons were made in this country as early as 1705, nine years before the accession of George I. besides which, the spoons brought from Hanover were probably of the florid type which prevailed in Germany and the Netherlands at this time (see fig. 66).

Early in George II's reign (1727-60), the rat-tail disappeared, and the entire back of the bowl, except the part adjoining the stem, was made quite plain. In place of the rat-tail, a miniature reproduction of the stem terminal, about half an inch in width and length appeared (see fig. 67).

Spoons of this variety continued to he made until nearly the middle of the eighteenth century, when several new forms of outline and ornamentation appear to have been introduced. The variety last described underwent a modification in its stem, the ridge and channel disappeared, except for about half an inch at the extreme end, where it curls forward. A 1753-4 spoon illustrates this modification.

But before the middle of the eighteenth century a new style of spoon was made which seems to have found much favour in some circles for about 30 years. It is a form known by silversmiths as the "Onslow" pattern (fig. 68), probably named after Arthur Onslow, Speaker of the House of Commons in the reign of George II. In earlier examples of this spoon, the bowl is typical of the contemporary spoon, with the double drop at the back; the outline of the ellipse is however more graceful, slightly wider near the stem, a little narrower at the point and the curve is smoother than in earlier spoons. But the stem is the remarkable feature of the "Onslow" pattern spoon for it is different

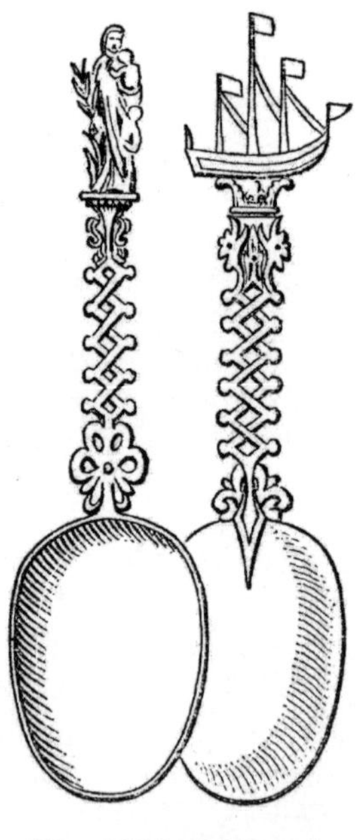

Fig. 66 Florid Dutch Spoons Length: 7.6in/19.2cm

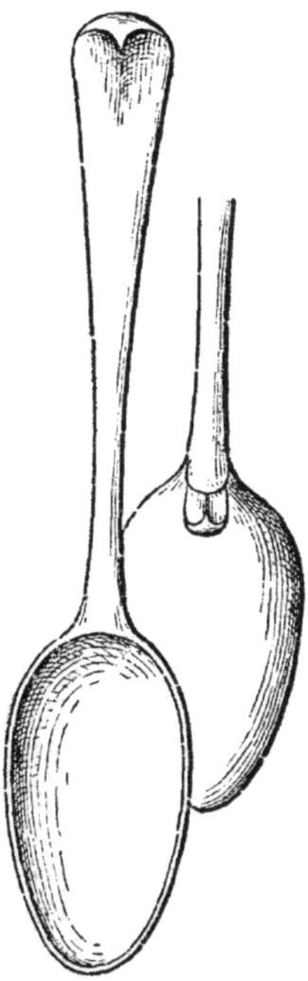

Fig. 67 "Rat-Tail" Disappearing Length: 8.1in/20.7cm

from every spoon, which preceded it in this country. Instead of being turned up at the end it is turned down and curled like an Ionic spiral, the upper side being moulded with a series of deeply-cut curved members which converge to a point about half-way down the stem. Two examples of this pattern of the years 1748-9 and 1772-3 have the double drop termination of the stem at the back of the bowl but in one of 1752-3 the lower drop is absent and a raised foliated scroll-ornament is substituted for it. This style of scroll-ornament is frequently found on the backs of spoons with stems of different form and of various dates but in most cases the stem is turned upwards. Sometimes a shell ornament, the ribs of which radiate from the drop, takes the place of the scroll on the back of the bowl, and in other instances the shell is surrounded by a scroll which extends half-way down the back of bowl.

The turned down end of the stem of the Onslow pattern spoon was the precursor of the general turning down which followed in the reign of George III (1760-1820) to the exclusion of the turned-up end, which by 1780 appears to have gone out of fashion. The spoon with the turned-down stem is known as the "Old English" pattern (fig. 70), which either plain or ornamented has been made almost continuously made for the last 240 years.

The succeeding "fiddle-pattern" spoon (fig. 71) and its numerous varieties, consisting of the plain, the threaded edge, the thread and shell, the lily and the nineteenth century ornate style known as the "king's" pattern (fig. 72) are still being made today. But there is one form of spoon (fig. 69) which lies midway between the eighteenth century "Old English" pattern and the nineteenth century "fiddle" pattern, which deserves mention. In essence it is "Old English" pattern but with the shoulders of the fiddle-pattern added on the stem near the bowl.

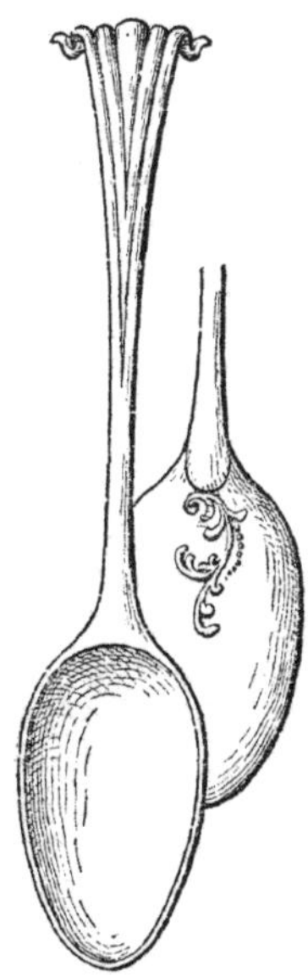

Fig. 68 "Onslow" Pattern Spoon Length: 8in/20.4cm

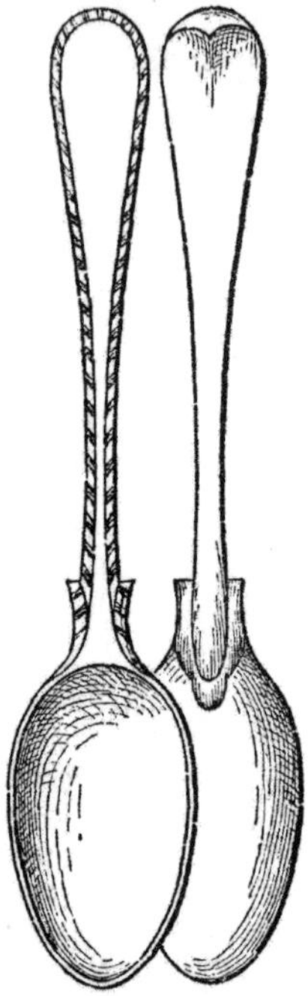

Fig. 69 Spoon with shouldered stem
Length: 8.6in/21.9cm

The stems of some eighteenth century spoons were made for other uses than that of handles. Tablespoons may be seen of various dates in the Georgian era with stems formed as marrow spoons which might have been used for the double purpose of an ordinary table spoon, and for extracting the marrow from a bone. A spoon of the year 1790-1 has both ends formed for extracting marrow from differently sized bones.

The teaspoon, like tea itself, is of comparatively modern introduction into Europe. Tea appears to have been imported into England soon after 1660 but it was regarded as a strange kind of herb for a number of years after and its drinking was for a considerable time used more on account of its medicinal properties than as an agreeable beverage. By the end of the seventeenth century however, it appears to have been consumed by the fashionable world in much the same manner as today but in smaller quantities, and sipped out of tiny cups which look like toys when compared with cups now in ordinary use.

The oriental teaspoon was of porcelain and it is not improbable that spoons, as well as cups and saucers of oriental porcelain, were brought to England with the introduction of tea. However, silver teaspoons were made in this country about the end of the seventeenth century. Small silver spoons of Charles II's (1660-85) time are sometimes called teaspoons but in most cases those are probably children's spoons or were used for eating eggs or sweetmeats. Considering the very small size and fragility of the very earliest teacups used in England, the small silver spoons dating earlier than the end of the seventeenth century will generally be found too heavy for that use.

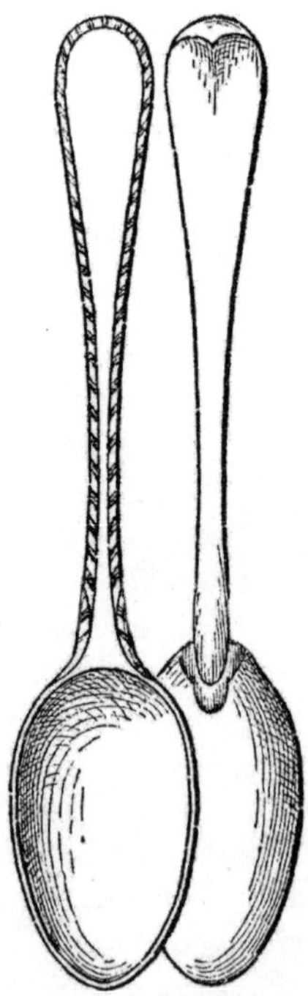

Fig. 70 "Old English Pattern" Spoon
Length: 8.6in/21.9cm

Fig. 71 Silver "Fiddle Pattern" Spoon, London 1860
Length: 5.7in/14.5cm

From the beginning, the form of the teaspoon appears to have followed that of the larger or tablespoon already described. The earliest have the flat split-end stem with rat-tail at the back of the bowl and the various changes, which succeeded that form, appear reflected in the smaller spoons of contemporary date.

The same may be said of the intermediate sized spoon, now called a "dessert" spoon, which appears to have come into use soon after 1660.

Also, in regard to base metal spoons, we see from numerous examples that from the earliest times, the fashion of the silver spoon was followed in the cheaper metals.

One type of spoon intimately associated with the once popular habit of snuff taking, which was introduced into England in the early eighteenth century as a result of the capture of vast quantities of snuff by Sir George Rooke in Vigo Bay. The manner in which many a fine lady and many a fine gentleman titillated their nostrils with the pungent dust required the use of the snuff-spoon, which was generally carried in an étui or trinket box. With the spoon a small quantity of snuff was extracted from the box, and either taken between the thumb and forefinger, or placed on the back of the left hand, when it was sniffed into the nostrils. The disagreeable sensation caused by the snuff getting under the fingernails in taking a pinch out of the box being thus avoided.

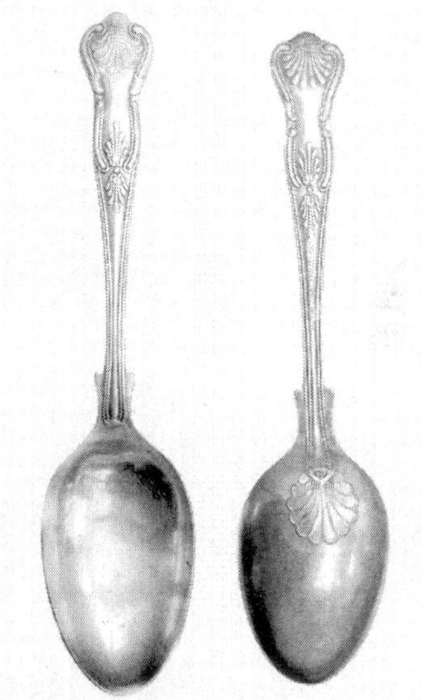

Fig. 72 EPNS "King's Pattern" Spoon, 20th Century
Length: 7.2in/18cm

Snuff-spoons were so very small that surviving examples are frequently mistaken for toy spoons. The earliest appear to be of the transitional type immediately following the split-ended stem of the beginning of the eighteenth century and they follow the styles of the larger spoons, both in stem and bowl, perfectly reproducing in miniature the tablespoon of the period.

There is a somewhat peculiar spoon of the eighteenth century, which has a perforated bowl and a round, long the stem, with a barbed and pointed end (fig. 73). Coming in three sizes – teaspoon to tablespoon, they are probably punch spoons. The perforated bowls were used for taking the floating cloves and lemon-pips off the surface of the liquor while the pointed and barbed end of the stem was used for fishing out the slices of lemon. The large spoon was used for the bowl, the intermediate size for the jug, and the smallest for the glass.

The origin of salt-spoons, like that of teaspoons, is fairly modern. They do not seem to have been used before the eighteenth century, and their form appears to have followed on a small scale that of larger spoons of contemporary date, at any rate as far as their stems were concerned. Their bowls are, however, generally round, or nearly so, except where they have been made in a fancy form which has had no appreciable effect upon any prevailing fashion.

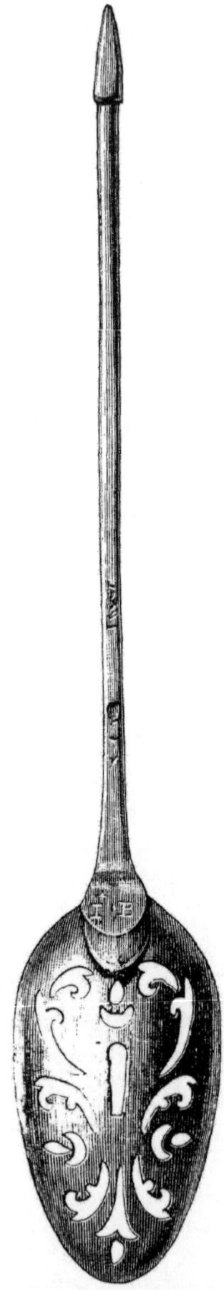

Fig. 73 Silver Punch Spoon with Perforated Bowl Length: 5.4in/13.6cm

OLD BASE METAL SPOONS

Base metal spoons must have been used in considerable numbers in the past. Every household in the country possessed some, yet few, if any have been kept and handed down. They seem to have been regarded as worthless trifles, used by the domestics of the household until worn out, and then thrown away or more probably sold to pewterers as scrap.

Such must have been their fate, as all our present collections of pewter and latten spoons have come from excavations, and those that are described and illustrated, with a few exceptions from rural sites, have been found in the City of London.

The marks have been arranged in chronological order according to the date or period of the style of the spoon, and at the end of the text on each type, all the known marks found on them are listed. By this means it should possible to find a date or period for some of the marks. The Pewterers' Company registers which had been kept since 1540, recording the names of members touches, have unfortunately been lost; it therefore becomes very difficult, if not impossible, to know to whom the touches belonged, and to determine exactly the date of any piece so stamped.

The later touch plates preserved by the Company, which have been illustrated in Charles Welch's *History of the Pewterers' Company*, bear comparatively few touches of spoonmakers whose marks can be identified. The earliest date that can be assigned to any mark upon these touch plates is about 1644, which is very late for the majority of the interesting old types. Silver spoons bearing date letters have proved invaluable for comparison with similar forms in base metal, and have enabled approximate dates to be assigned in many cases. It may be taken for granted that all the known silver types were reproduced in pewter or latten as soon as such particular forms came into fashion, but there are a few patterns which are not known to occur in silver.

As instances of those unknown in silver, there is the 'horned head-dress' knop, a rare elegant fifteenth century type. Also the 'baluster' knop, not to be confused with the baluster stalked spoon with the seal on the top. Of several others having curious knops only single specimens are known such as the 'Chantieleer,' the 'Stagshead,' the 'Globe,' and perhaps others.

To begin the study of base metal spoons it is notable that nearly all English examples, whether made of base metal or silver, from the 14th century to the mid-17th century, had fig-shaped bowls curving upwards, being broader at the base and narrower near the stalk or stem. The stems were 'six-squared' or hexagonal, and terminated mostly with a knop, varying according to existing fashion or the whim of the spoonmaker.

The earliest pewter spoon known to have been found in London is a 'Ball knop' (fig. 4). It may be earlier than the fine stalked, slender spoons made of latten, a variety of brass, called 'Cones' and 'Finials,' which are probably foreign and date 14th or early 15th century.

Before the 14th century, with the exception of this 'Ball knop' no English pewter spoons are known although they may have been made and not survived. Earlier spoons in ordinary domestic use were probably made either of wood or horn and the wealthier made use of imported latten spoons. The usual types of spoons such as those knopped with Acorns, Diamond Points, 'Maidenheads,' Horned Head-dresses, Hexagons, Apostles, Writhen balls, Sitting Lions, Balusters, Sealtops, Strawberries or 'de Fradeletts,' some of which were occasionally gilded, were probably not made in England before the end of the 14th or beginning of the 15th century. Early in the 16th century a very simple type of spoon came into use, often described in wills and inventories as 'Slipped in the Stalk.' These had the usual fig-shaped bowl, and an hexagonal stem with the top cut off at an angle from the front of the spoon. This type, judging from the large quantity found in London, must have been very popular, and from its simplicity was the cheapest form. It remained in fashion well into the middle of the 17th century, when the bowls became broader near the stem and narrower at the base, and the stems flatter and only four-sided. This form again changed about 1650, when the stems were hammered out flatter, widening out from the bowl to the end, which had two or three small nicks cut but otherwise terminating quite square. This type is called the 'Puritan' and many are found in both pewter and latten. From the 'Puritan' spoon another type naturally developed having the same shaped bowl, with a still flatter stem but with the end beaten out much broader and ornamented with two deep cuts and on the back of the bowl, a tongue or rat-tail. This type became popular about 1663 and is known as the 'Split End' or 'Pied de Biche', of which there are a great many varieties. The type continued in use until the end of the 17th century when another type was evolved called the 'Wavy End.' This is a spoon with a long narrow bowl and a longer stem with a flat tongued or shield-like end, terminating in a hook. By 1714, a type called the 'Rounded End' came into fashion which lasted until the late 18th century when modern types of spoon came into use.

Pewter spoons having latten knops are uncommon and date to the latter part of the 16th century. A Court of the Pewterers' Company held 4 January, 1562/3, refers to these latten knopped spoons: 'Stephin Calie complayned agaynst Richarde Harrysson for 15lb of fyne mettall which after the price of 6d. the pounde is 7s. 6d. the same Harrysson hathe promysed to paye unto the said Stephin every weke 2 dosen of Spones with latten knobbes untill the said mony were Ron owt.' This suggests that Harryson was perhaps the inventor of this special type of spoon.

The spoonmakers also sometimes gilded the knops of pewter spoons and a few specimens still exist.

The precise composition of the pewter used for spoons is difficult to define without analysis, as they were doubtless made of different alloys.

'Fine Pewter' (English) contained 81% tin and 19% copper.

'Better pewter' of the highest quality had 89% tin, 7% antimony and 4% copper. There are many other qualities of pewter ware such as 'Trifle' or common pewter consisting of 83% tin and 17% antimony, also a second quality of the same consisted of 82% tin and 18% antimony. This trifle metal or plate metal was probably used by the spoonmakers, who were most likely a distinct branch of the pewterer's craft. Yet at one time, 'Triflers' worked in trifle metal and plate metal on lighter wares such as spoons and, later on, forks, buckles, toys and buttons but by 1612, they were making much hollow-ware.

At a Court of the Pewterers' Company held 16 December, 1669, it was enacted: 'That the Order made ye 19th Dec: 1667 That the spoone-maker should receive from the shopkeeper (for all spoones they delivered them after christmas then next following) all plate mettle shall be made null & void, and that they receive such mettle as the Hollow-ware men & of noe other sort'.

A careful analysis of latten and pewter spoons shows:

Latten, early 17th century:		***Latten, second half 17th century:***	
Copper	72.50%	Copper	73.33 %
Zinc	25.22%	Zinc	24.80%
Iron	1.82%	Iron	2.15%

Pewter, late 16th century or early 17th century:

Tin	97.00 %	Tin	95.60 %
Lead	1.65%	Lead	3.64%
Copper	1.42%	Copper	1.06%

With the exception of the 'Cone' and 'Finial' types latten spoons probably were not made in England before the second quarter of the 16th century and a few of the old pewter shapes were probably never produced in latten. The earliest known types, excluding the above, made in latten appear to have been Acorns, Apostles, Seal tops, and 'Slipped in the Stalks.'

After the middle of the 16th century it seems that brass or latten spoons were encroaching upon the trade of the pewter spoonmakers, as we find that at the Court of the Pewterers' Company on the 23 September, 1567-8: "it was agreed by the whole Company that there shoulde Be no spones made of Bras or latten or any yelow metall uppon payne that if any person herafter be found that he doth make any suche spones shall forfeyt and pay for every spone 3s. 4d."

"The said Spones were lately Invented by John God And he hath confessed he hath made but 3 dosen one dosen he hath solde to one at Algate And an other Stranger hath bought one other dosen And the third dosen the Goodman of the Castell in wood strete must have them And if there be found any more of the same God makyng He shall pay for every Spone 3s. 4d."

And again we find the following in 1586-7: "At this court [14 June] it is determyned that all the makers of lattyn sponnes in London shalbe warned the next court day and that thay shal be bound to make no more sponnes."

"At this court (4 August) comaundement was geven unto the spovnmakers accordyng to ane ordynance hertofore made that yf any spone maker doth make any short lattyn spounes or of yallow mettall shall forfayt for every spone 3s. 4d. as may appeare by the former order upon Which comaundement the spounmakers promysed to be obedyent to the same or els to be fyned wheruppon they have set ther handes."

These stringent regulations must have greatly impeded latten spoon-making for some time and may be the cause of the very few specimens that appear to be 16th century. There are specimens of 'Seal tops' and 'Slipped in the Stalks' spoons known in latten, marked:  which may possibly be the mark of John God mentioned earlier.

It is probable that the regulations set out in the 16th century that no spoons should be made of latten were relaxed during the first quarter of the 17th century, as latten spoonmakers increased very rapidly in numbers during that period. The superior advantages of the latten spoon undoubtedly alarmed the Company who dreaded the general substitution, of them for their pewter.

Pewter spoons frequently appear to have been gilded but, as analysis proves the total absence of gold, this is probably only surface oxidation through the spoons having been buried in the soil for centuries.

Some spoons occasionally show the remains of lacquering but the gilding of pewter was strictly prohibited by the Pewterers' Company, as the following minute of a Court held 3rd July 1623 testifies:

"The Master acquainted the Court of the search about ye painted pewter and for the Contempt they have taken Course of lawe, and albeit some of the makers or gilders did promise to desist from sellinge the same, yett they doe sett upp Bills for the sale of the same."

This painted pewter is probably what we should now call lacquered.

The following are interesting extracts about pewter spoons from the minutes of the Pewterers' Company: 1580, 13 December: "the woorkmanshype of halfe a grose of spones at 10d. the half grose."

1582: " At court beinge quarter daye held the 5 december 1582 It was ordered that none of the companye shuld put to make any spones but unto a brother of the company and all the spone makers promysed in open court to worke a grose of spones for 20d. the grose." 1588: "At this court (1 November) it is ordered betwyxt mr wood and John bowyar that he shall worke unto mr wood 2 grose of sponnes aweeke at 18d. the grose untyll such tyme all his debt be wrought out and yf in case he fayleth then mr wood to be at his lyberty."

1662: "Ordered by this Court [11 December] that all Laymen doe alter there tutches within fourteens dayes with ye date of 1663." This order was undoubtedly observed, as the marks of E.H., I.H., and W.A., on 'Slipped in the Stalks' spoons bear 63 on their touches as well as initials.

1666-7: at this Court [21 March] wm Austin affirmed mrs Johnson usually mixt in her mettle for Spoons glasiers knotts [lead].

On 20 June, 1667, Robert Wheely was fined 5s. for the bad quality of his turning spoons. To remedy the bad quality of metal used in making spoons it was decided (19 December) "to convert all spoons into Lay as they Come to any mans hands or Custody between this & Christmas, and from thence every Shopkeeper or other to deliver unto ye spoon maker plate mettle or as good." It was also ordered that "everie Spoon maker shall alter his touch imediately after christmas next from Which tyme all Spoons shall be made exactly to ye Say."

1677, 13 December-"Ordered that all planished ware and squarework which is wrought by the hand and all round Fyne Chamber-potts and new-ffashioned spoones shall henceforward be made of good ffyne plate mettle." Evidently early pewter spoons were made by hammering and beating and made by men whose sole business was spoonmaking.

Notwithstanding the stringent Company rules against spoonmakers for making their spoons by means of an 'engine,' clearly they continued to do so acording to the following extracts from the Company's proceedings.

1683: "Daniel Barton complained [20 December] against John Clark Thomas Waight & Joseph Higdon for makeing spoones wthout beating being only cast grated & burnished." However the spoonmakers complained, 7 April 1686-7, of Mr. Barton for using an 'engine' to make spoons. He convinced the Court that his spoons were well-finished and undertook not to sell them under six shillings a gross, in the country and four in town. "which will be noe prejudice to ye other workemen."

1691, 17 December: John French was complained of "for Grateing Spoons and not beat."

1695-6: it was ordered on 19 March that all spoons should in future be beaten and not grated and burnished only. Undoubtedly moulds were employed, and a stone mould for casting Seal-top spoons from the early 17th century, marked W.M. has been found. Slight variations occur in some of the marks which appear to be those of the same spoonmaker but slightly differentiated, perhaps indicating that new punches had to be made to replace old ones when they had become worn, or that the spoonmaker had received orders from the Company to alter his mark, as was the case in 1661-2 and in 1666-7. Sometimes the differences are only the addition or the omission of a couple or more dots, placed under or over the initials, or a plain circle replacing a dotted circle. In the case of the maker R.A., who used two keys in his touch, the key bowls are sometimes apart and at others they join or even overlap. It is very difficult to say whether these differences are accidental or intentional.

There are a few marks in which the initials are enclosed in a dotted lozenge. These perhaps indicate that the spoonmaker was a woman, as was the case with silversmiths.

Those marks which are found within square-topped shields invariably belong to the latter half of the 17th century.

The marks in the bowls of these base metal spoons are usually read by holding the spoon by the stem, with the knop or end pointing to the body of the person holding it; occasionally the reverse is the case.

Thus, if we take one mark for instance, and look at it in the usual way with the end of the stem pointing to the body, it reads N.I., but if looked at the reverse way, we find it is I.N. This is somewhat misleading, but there is very little doubt that the initials are N.I. There are several other makers whose initials are reversible, whose marks are given in this book, which have been read in the manner indicated. As the register of marks has been lost it is now impossible to ascertain the makers' names.

The 'spoonsmark' was a very favourite device for latten spoonmakers in their touches, and a great variety of them are listed. It may be presumed that they were first adopted about the time of Charles II. It is a singular circumstance that none of the latten spoonmakers appear to have used in his mark the key which was so common with the pewter spoonmakers, whereas the pewter spoons are not found with 'spoonmarks' on them before the middle of the 17th century, and only a few makers adopted them then.

The earliest base metal spoons that were in use in London, probably during the latter part of the 14th and 15th centuries, and that have survived to our time, are those long slender stemmed specimens of very elegant shape, made of latten, which are described as 'Cones' and 'Finials.'

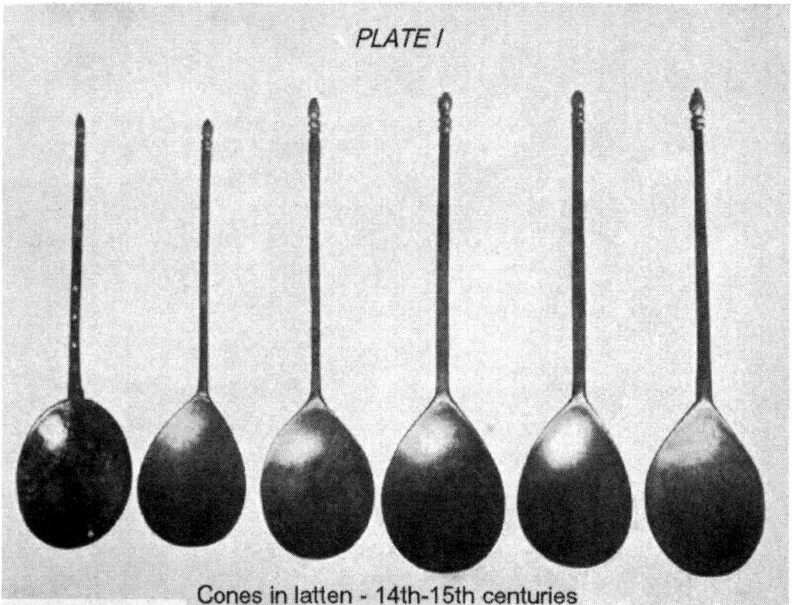

Approx. 40% actual size

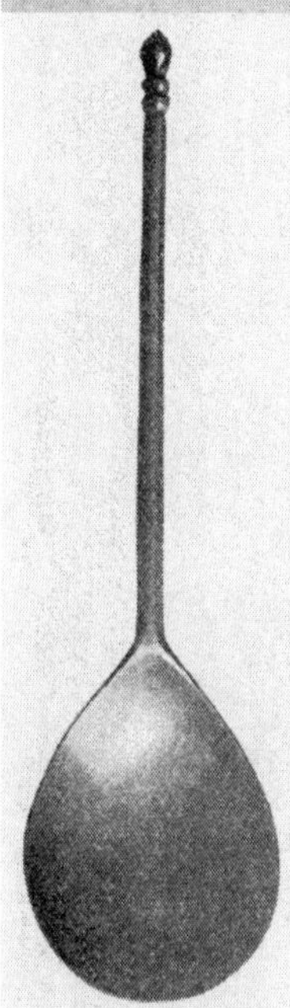

Fig. 1 Latten Spoon with Cone End Length: 6.75in/17cm

CONES

These spoons, which are always made of latten, have fig-shaped bowls and long thin stems of diamond section, terminating in a small knop representing what may be intended to be a fir-cone or pineapple. They are usually marked on the back of the bowl with a small punch, of which some of the marks are given here.

Fig. 1 is dated late 14th or early 15th century. *See* Plate I. A very small specimen of a latten spoon of this type, 2.9 inches or 7.3 centimetres in length is also known.

FINIALS

These are in every respect, of the same shape and size as the Cones with the exception that the stems end with a Finial for a knop, some of which are larger than others. They vary from 6.5in/16.5cm to 7.5in/19cm in length. They are also marked on the backs of the bowls in a similar manner to the Cones.

There is a fine specimen of a two-pronged fork, 6.75in/17cm long, of the same pattern as the spoon, which is also said to have been found in London. *See* Plate II. This is an unusually early date for a fork made of latten. Forks are occasionally mentioned in inventories of the 14th-15th centuries, but they are generally described as 'for eating green ginger.'

There is another early form of latten spoon, with a round bowl, the stem flat near the bowl and tapering towards the end, which terminates in a tiny knop. They are marked on the upper side of the flat stem:

sometimes with two touches, these may be French and belong to the late 14th-15th centuries. See Plate VIII, fig. 3.

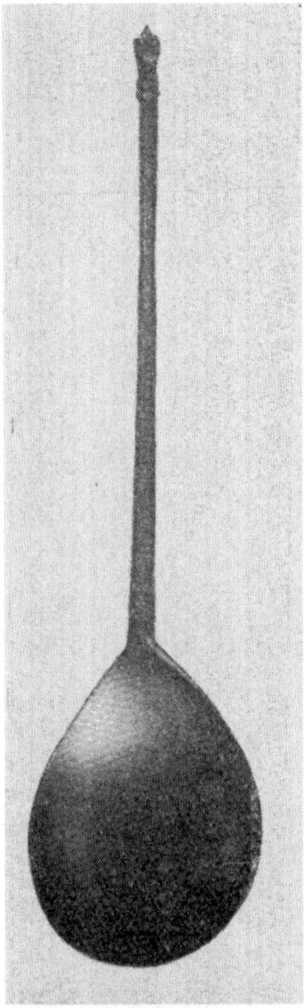

Fig. 2 Spoon with Finial Top Length: 6.75in/17cm

Marks on Cones:

Marks on Finials:

A pewter Finial spoon is known with a round bowl, a long slender hexagonal stem, rather flattened at the bowl and having a slight indication of a mark, which is indecipherable. The stem terminates in a finial, which is made of brass or latten. It was found in London and is remarkably similar to French silver spoons of about 1330 (fig. 3).

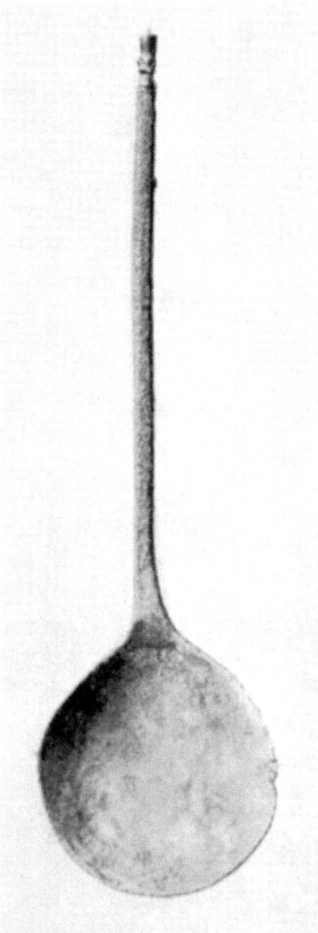

Fig. 3 Pewter Finial Spoon with brass or latten top Length: 6.9in/17.5cm

Another example ends with what may be called a Ball knop but this is simply a provisional name, as it appears to be quite a new variety. It is of a most unusual shape for a pewter spoon, and is the earliest known type in that metal. The stem is similar to latten spoons termed 'Cones' and 'Finials' (fig. 4).

There is a similar Ball-knopped Spoon with a small mark in the bowl, which does not appear to be complete, and another, which is furnished with a ball near the centre of the stem in addition to the knop. This spoon, has a small leaf-shaped bowl, being more pointed at the base than the latter types, with a long slender rounded stem, terminating in a small ball knop. It has no mark and was found in Westminster. It is probably 13th or 14th century. There is also a similar shaped spoon, which has a ball on the stem in addition to the knop.

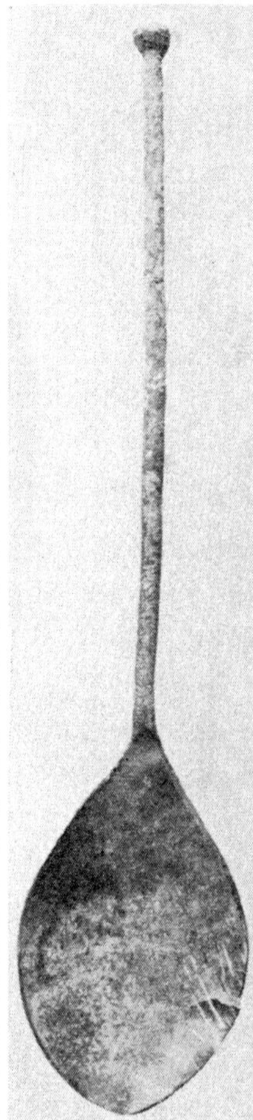

Fig. 4 Ball-knopped Spoon Length: 6.9in/17.5cm

ACORN KNOPS

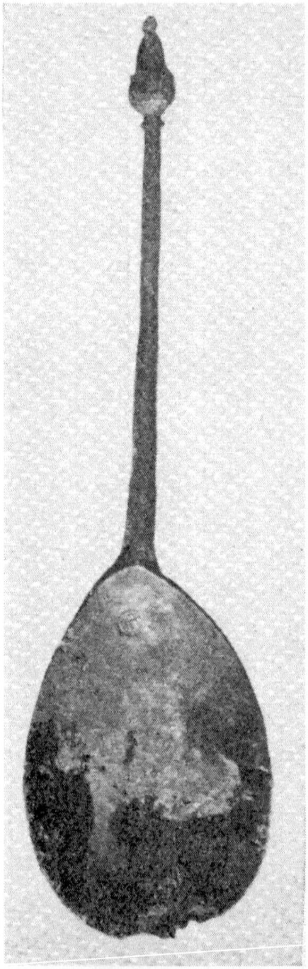

Fig. 5 Acorn-knopped Spoon
Length: 6.5in/16.5cm

These are generally considered to be the earliest forms of pewter spoons (as they are in silver). They have small fig-shaped bowls with very slender stems, generally somewhat rounded, furnished at the end with a small acorn. Occasionally very small examples are found, having a four-sided or diamond section stem. These are probably early 16th century or perhaps a little earlier.

There is another form of these spoons, which are larger, having a bigger acorn with the same shaped bowl and the stems often quite round. They all bear the touch of the spoon-maker in the bowl, and are probably 14th or 15th century.

The earliest specimen known is a latten example (*see* Plate II) with a long stem, knopped with an elongated acorn, of the same type as the 'Cones' and 'Finials' ascribed to the 14th century. It is seven inches (17.8cm) long and unmarked. The first mention of this form of knop known is to be found in a will of 1348 proved at the Court of Husting in 1351, whereby John de Holegh bequeathed to Thomas Taillour, twelve silver spoons with *akernes* and again in a will of 1361, John Botiller, draper, bequeathed to Isabella, his wife, twelve best spoons with gilt acorns. Also in a will dated 1392, registered at York, six silver spoons 'with gold acorns' are mentioned.

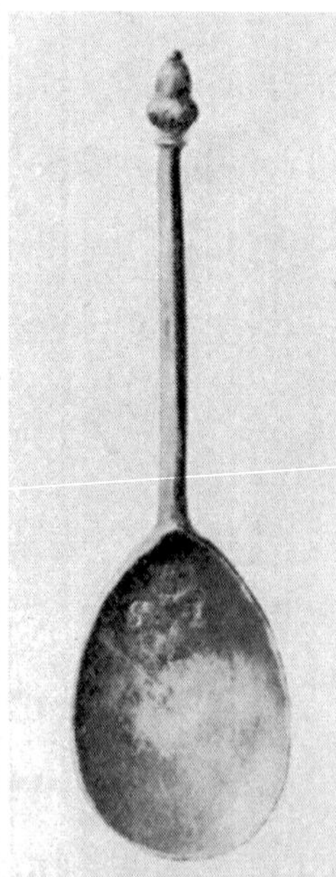

Fig. 6 Unusually small Acorn-knopped Spoon
Length: 5.1in/13cm

In an inventory of plate belonging to the Cathedral Church of Lincoln, taken in 1548, there appear the following:
"A Spoone with an Akerne; ordeined for Creame." "A Spoone With an Akerne: ordeined for *holy oil*" and "a Spoone, haveing an Akerne of ye end: ordeined for *oil [Infirmary]*" but these examples of course, were much earlier than the date of the inventory. Some of the very small spoons of this type in pewter may well be as early as the latter part of the 14th century or beginning of the 15th century.

There is a very small-sized pewter spoon marked: 
in the bowl between T and S, evidently the initials of a former owner (fig. 6). This is unusually early for ownership marks. The spoon dates to the 16th century. There is a smaller spoon that is only 3.6 inches (9.1cm) long.

Marks on Acorn knopped spoons:

Mark on a latten Acorn, probably John God: 

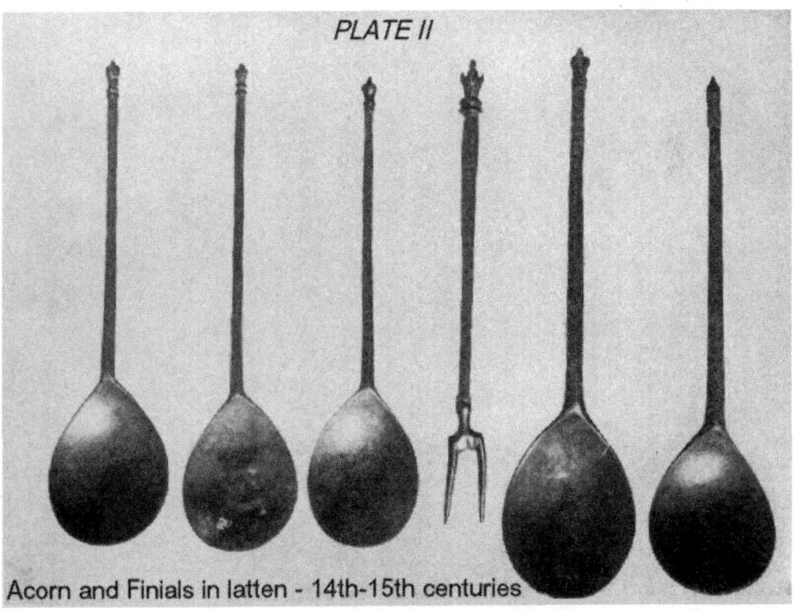

PLATE II

Acorn and Finials in latten - 14th-15th centuries

Approx. 40% actual size

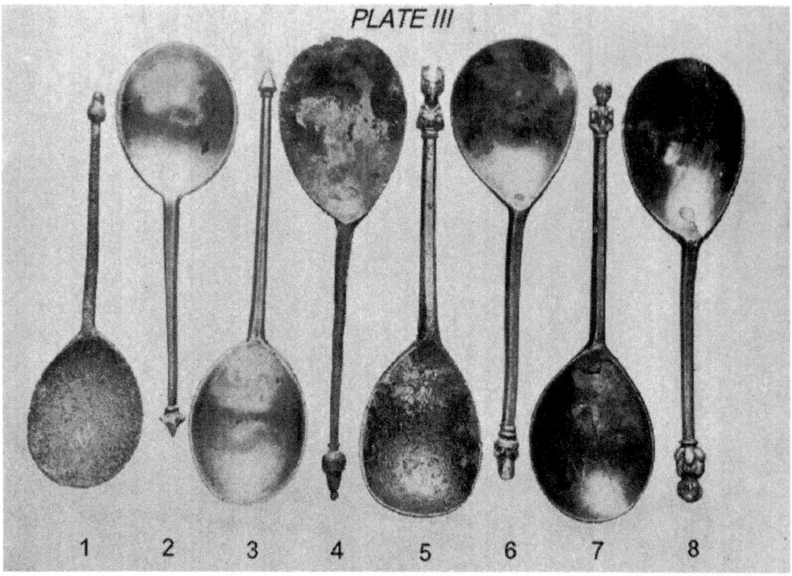

NOTES TO PLATE III

All pewter. Approx. 40% actual size

1. Acorn knop: no mark. 15th century.
2. Diamond Point: no mark. 15th century.
3. Diamond Point: no mark. 15th century.
4. Acorn knop 14th-15th century, mark:

5. Horned-headed dress: no mark; early 15th century.

6. Maidenhead knop 15th century, mark:

7. Maidenhead knop 15th century, mark:

8. Maidenhead knop 15th century, mark:

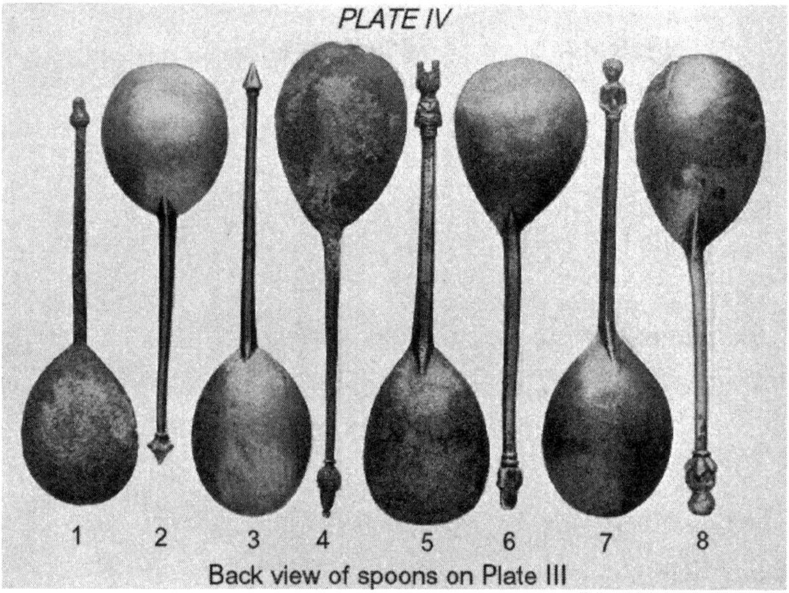

Approx. 40% actual size

HORNED HEAD DRESS KNOP

This is a very rare type of spoon. It is of somewhat slender make, the bowl fig-shaped, and the stalk or stem hexagonal or 'six-squared.' The knop represents the bust of a woman wearing the peculiar horned or horseshoe form of head-dress which was fashionable in the reigns of Henry V and Henry VI (fig. 7). This form of spoon probably dates to the first half of the 15th century.

Out of about a dozen of these spoons known, only two of them bear a mark:

they are unknown in silver.

Fig. 7 may be a variety of the Maidenhead type to be described shortly.

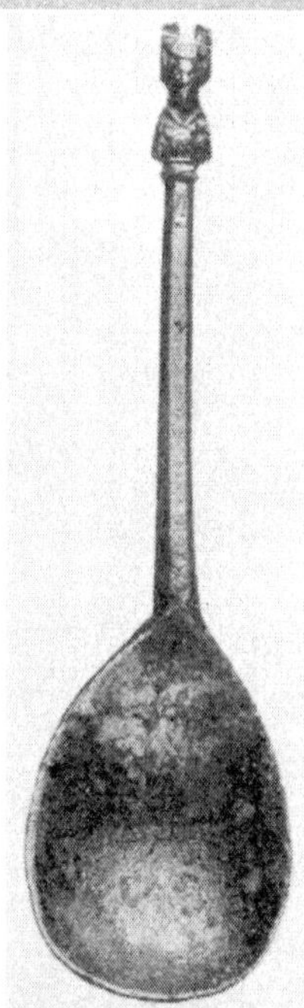

Fig. 7 Spoon with Horned Head Dress Knop Length: 6.3in/16cm

DIAMOND POINT

Spoons with Diamond pointed knops or Hexagonal Spearheads are very rare in pewter, and it is doubtful whether they were ever made in latten. They have round fig-shaped bowls, and hexagonal stems terminating with an hexagonal spear or diamond pointed knop.

A peculiar form found in the Thames at London has a flattened diamond shaped knop, having a depression in the centre, with a round stem ornamented at the lower end; the bowl is furnished with a tongue behind and has ornamentation on each side of it. From the Lombardic M in the bowl, it may be from the first half of the 14th century but it is probably much later. *See* Plate VIII.

Spoons terminating in the diamond knop are probably 14th and 15th centuries.

The earliest silver example mentioned is in an inventory of Robert Morton of the year 1487 and we may assume that pewter examples are also from that period.

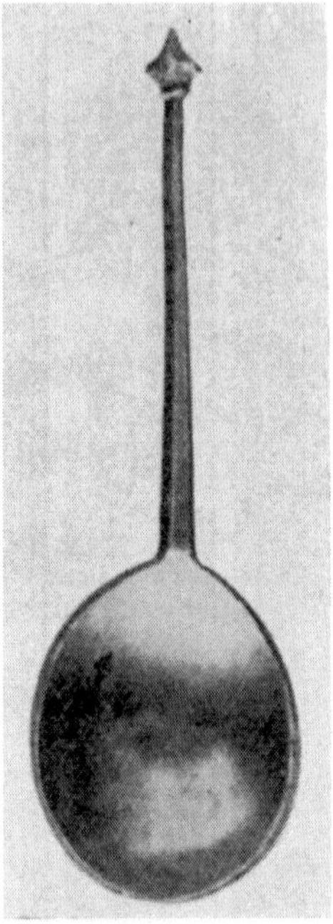

Fig. 8 Spoon with Diamond Pointed Knop
Length: 5.5in/14cm

The earliest specimen known is a silver one with a long fig-shaped bowl and unusually short stem, unmarked but considered to date around 1400.

This type of pewter spoon does not appear to have been marked, perhaps because of its early date.

There is a very small spoon with a fig-shaped bowl: the stem is of a diamond section, ending in a sort of embryo diamond point with a small ring fixed to the point (fig. 8a). This little spoon cannot be later than the 16th century, and probably dates from the 15th century, as it was found in Worship Street, Shoreditch, with other objects, all of that period.

This spoon was probably made as a toy and may be the smallest early example known. It has no mark, has been made in a mould and the edges have not been trimmed.

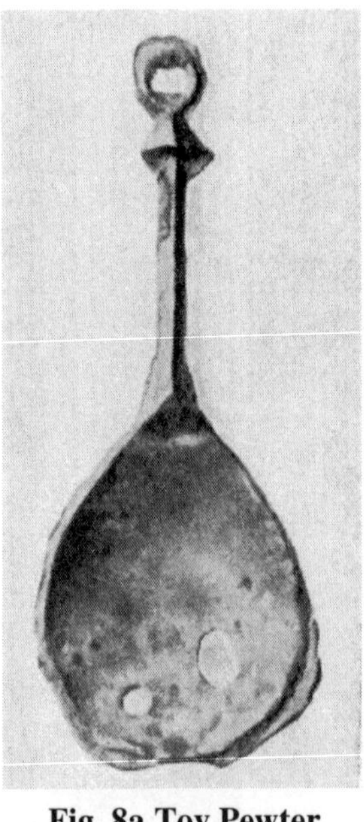

Fig. 8a Toy Pewter Spoon
Length: 2.4in/6cm

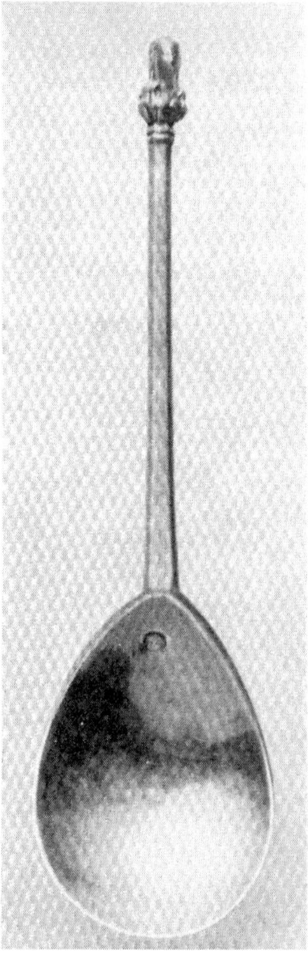

Fig. 9 Spoon with Maidenhead Knop Length: 6in/15.5cm

MAIDENHEAD KNOP

This is another early form of spoon. The bowl is somewhat fig-shaped, and the stem is hexagonal, terminating in a knop representing the bust of a maiden, perhaps the Blessed Virgin (fig. 9).

These spoons were made of pewter probably as early as the 15th century; they were certainly in use during the 16th century.

The earliest published reference to silver 'maidenhead spoons' occurs in an inventory of Durham Priory dated 1446.

A silver spoon of this type, bearing the London date letter for 1631, which is a very late date for this type, had possibly been made to supply a missing spoon in a set, or may have been made for a member of the Mercers' Company, whose badge is a Maidenhead.

Marks on Maidenhead knopped spoons:

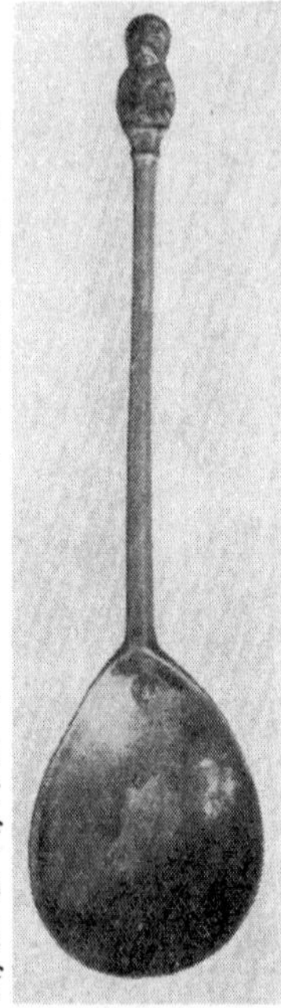

Fig. 10 Spoon with Monk's Head Knop Length: 7.4in/18.8cm

MONK'S HEAD KNOP

This is an unusual form of knop and may easily be mistaken for a 'Maidenhead.' The only one in pewter known, which dates to the early part of the 16th century, has a fig-shaped bowl, the stem at the bowl end is somewhat hexagonal in section but it becomes round and ends at the top with a cowled head of a monk; his hands folded in front of him (fig. 10). The stem of this spoon is unusually long; in the bowl is an engraved Maltese Cross, presumably an owners mark, as the touch in the bowl is:

Brass spoons of this type have been found in London and two specimens found in the Thames have fig shaped bowls which are much smaller than the pewter spoon. One is furnished with a tongue upon the back of the bowl, and the other has six dots in lieu of it; the stems are round and are ornamented with a sort of baluster; the knops are the same as that on the pewter spoon just described. They are unmarked. These spoons date from early in the 16th century and are probably of foreign origin. See Plate X.

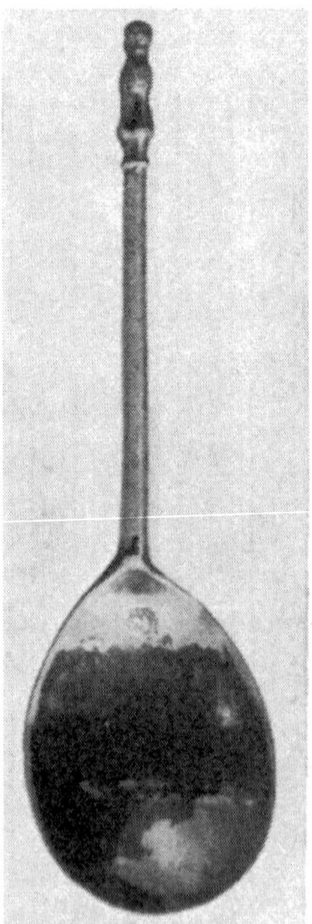

Fig. 11 Spoon with Sitting Lion Knop Length: 6.25in/16cm

SITTING LION KNOP

This is another 16th century form of spoon. They have fig-shaped bowls, hexagonal stems, and are knopped with a sitting lion. Very few are known in pewter. A small-sized spoon is marked:

in the bowl and appears to have been lacquered (fig. 11). Specimens in latten are occasionally found but are uncommon and date to the 17th century.

Marks on pewter spoons:

Marks on latten spoons:

WRITHEN KNOPS

Fig. 12 Writhen Knopped Spoon Length: 5.6in/14.2cm

Writhen knops are very rare in any metal. They are first mentioned in silver about the year 1488, so we may assume that this type was made in pewter during the whole period of the 16th century.

The form of the spoon is the same as those already mentioned, but the knop is composed of a ball, spirally twisted; occasionally it is elongated or elliptical. These knops were sometimes gilded. S*ee* Plate VIII, fig. 9. One small pewter spoon has an elongated twisted knop made of latten or brass.

There is a very unusual 16th century spoon of this type, with a fig-shaped bowl and twisted stem, the knop being, as usual, spirally fluted.

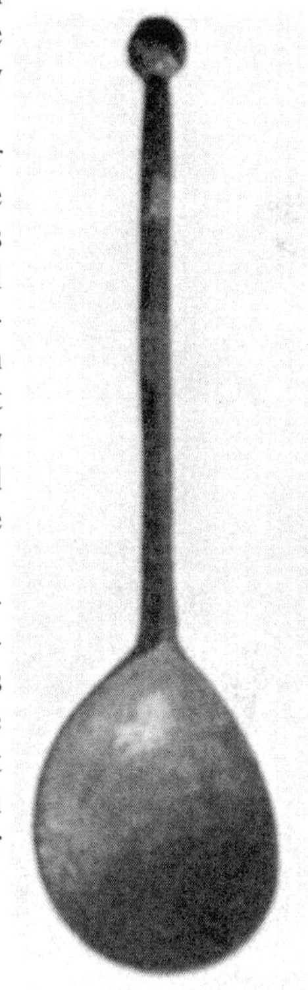

Fig. 13 Writhen Knopped Bronze Spoon Length: 7.5in/18.5cm

There is also another curious example of this type of spoon in pewter which has the usual fig-shaped bowl with an ornamental baluster-shaped stem, with a writhen knop; it is unmarked, most probably foreign and very similar in style to a so-called Strawberry knop, on Plate VIII, fig. 6.

A most unusual specimen (fig. 13) has a fig-shaped bowl and a long diamond section stem, terminating in a writhen knop. It is unmarked, appears to be made of bronze, and strongly resembles the 'Cone' and 'Finial' types already described; in fact if it was latten and more slender, it would have been classed with them. It probably belongs to the 14th or 15th century.

Marks found on Writhen knop spoons:

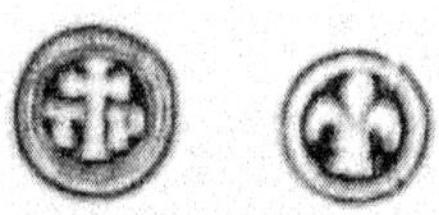

MELON OR LOBED KNOP

This is another type of the same form of spoon with a fig-shaped bowl and hexagonal stem, terminating with a knop vertically fluted or lobed instead of the spirally twisted or writhen knop; it may thus be described as being like a melon. Pewter specimens are occasionally found in London, but are uncommon. One is illustrated here of 17th century date and is unmarked (fig. 14).

Another spoon has the mark:

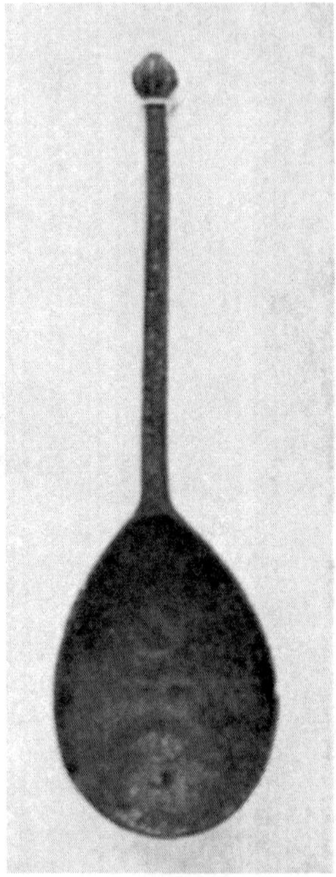

Fig. 14 Melon Knopped Spoon
Length: 6.25in/16cm

HEXAGONAL OR SIX-SQUARED KNOPS

Hexagonal or six-squared knops, are frequently found in pewter but they are extremely rare in latten. They have fig-shaped bowls, with stout six-sided or hexagonal stems, terminating in a 'six-squared' knop, not unlike a crown. This type of spoon is rarely found in silver, the only one known bearing the date letter for 1480.

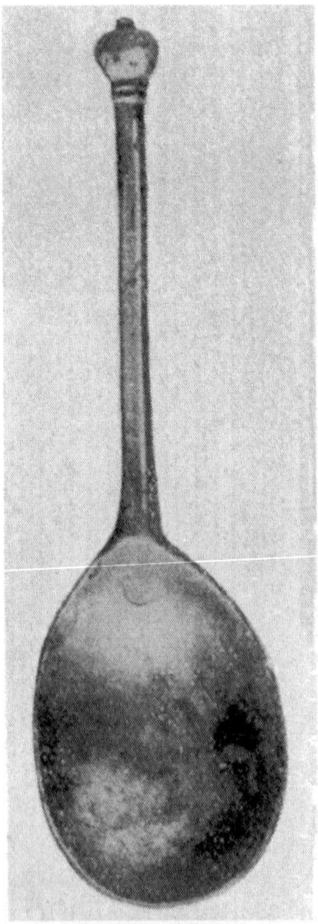

Fig. 15 Hexagonal Knopped Spoon.
Length: 6.3in/16cm

This type of spoon did not remain long in fashion, assuming that the pewter forms came into vogue during the first half of the 16th century; they probably went out of fashion by the end of it.

A considerable number are listed in the inventory of spoons possessed by King Henry VIII.

Marks:

APOSTLE KNOPS

Fig. 16 Pewter Apostle Spoon
Length: 7in/17.6cm

These came into fashion late in the 15th century and remained in vogue throughout the 16th and the first half of the 17th century, after which time they were seldom made until more recently.

Examples in pewter are somewhat rare.

The bowls are fig-shaped, with stout hexagonal stems, knopped with the figure of an apostle but without a halo (fig. 16).

They are more frequently found in latten, and the ordinary specimens have rounder bowls, with thin four-sided stems with a groove running up the middle. A more substantial type is sometimes found with a short fig-shaped bowl marked:

this spoon has been tinned and gilded; but many Apostle spoons in latten are even of later date, especially those bearing spoons in the touches.

Marks on pewter spoons:

Marks on latten spoons:

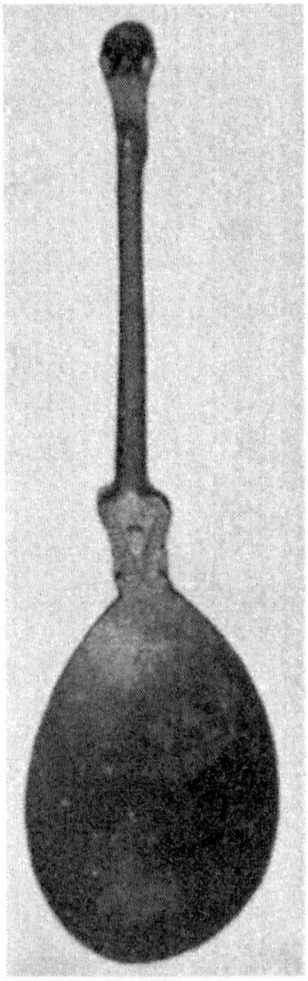

Fig. 17 Spoon with Horsehoof Knop Length: 6.5in/16.5cm

HORSEHOOF KNOP

This is a rare form of spoon, the bowl is fig-shaped with an ornamental shoulder near the bowl, a rounded stem, terminating with the hoof of a horse, showing a very well-formed shoe (fig. 17). Several are known in pewter and date to the 16th or early 17th century. There are also some in latten but mostly of a different shape, bearing other marks and the hoofs are not so well defined as those in pewter; they have been found in London and are probably of French origin.

A specimen of this type in silver bears a date letter for 1652.

Marks:

(in the bowl of a latten spoon of exactly the same pattern as fig. 17).

STUMP END

This is another form of 16th century spoon, and very rare, though also known in silver. It has a fig-shaped bowl, with a rounded stem, increasing slightly in thickness from the bowl to the end, when it terminates abruptly. The spoon illustrated (fig. 18) is pewter with a maker's mark in the bowl:

This type is unknown in latten. Two examples of Stump End spoons found in London, one of which has a very thick stem with a fig-shaped bowl, with a merchant's mark in the bowl in addition to the pewterer's touch is 16th century. The other spoon, dating about 1695, has the same kind of stout stem furnished with a tongue or rat-tail, and is Dutch, the former is also probably foreign.

Marks:

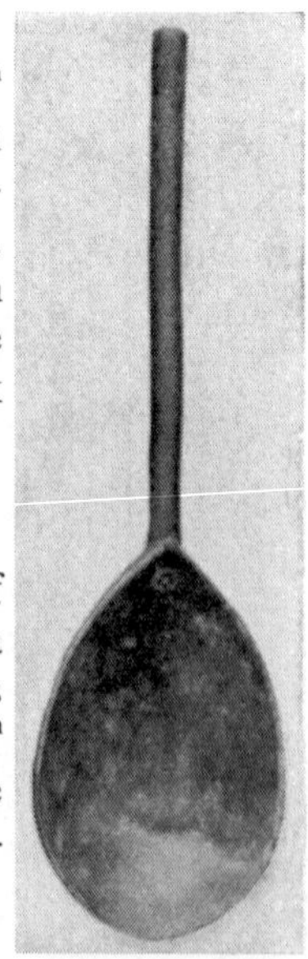

Fig. 18 Stump-end Spoon Length: 6.25in/16cm

BALUSTER KNOPS

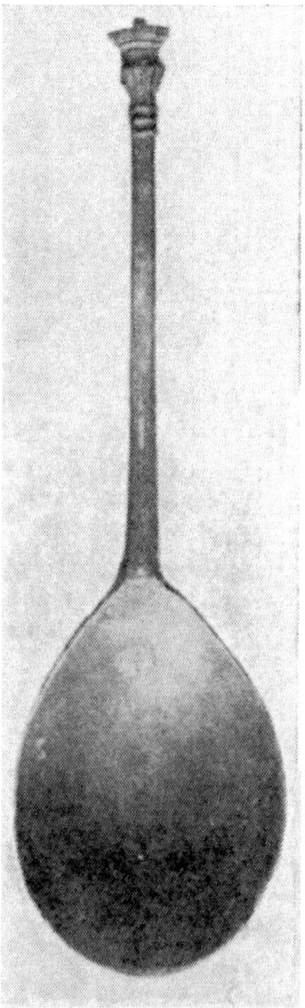

Fig. 19 Baluster-Knopped Spoon Length; 5.9in/15cm

This form of pewter spoon has the usual fig-shaped bowl and hexagonal stem, terminating with a baluster at the end, with a small button or knop at the top of it. It is often confused with the Seal Top spoon but it is quite different. Inasmuch as the Seal Top has a flattened seal at the end of the baluster stem, it may be considered as being the precursor of the baluster knop. There is an unusually small specimen of this type shown in Plate X.

Examples are often found in pewter, which probably date to the 16th century. Those made of latten are from the second half of the 17th century and are rare. There is another form of the Baluster, which only occurs in pewter (see fig. 20); it has a fig-shaped bowl and hexagonal stem with an elongated baluster knop, without the flattened disc and button at the end. This type is of elegant design and very rare. It was probably made in the latter half of the 16th century.

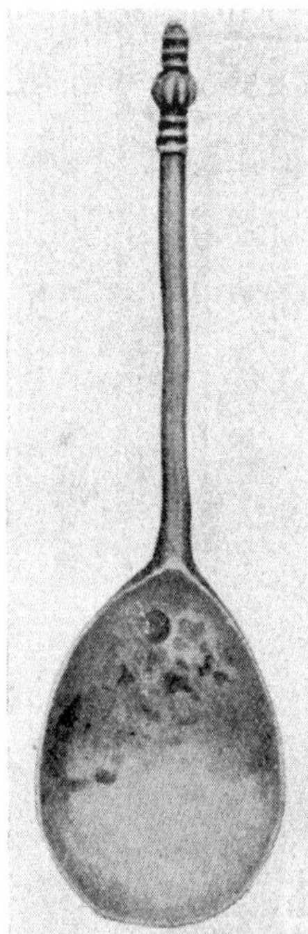

Fig. 20 Pewter Baluster-Knopped Spoon Length:

Marks on Pewter Baluster Knops:

Marks on Latten Spoons:

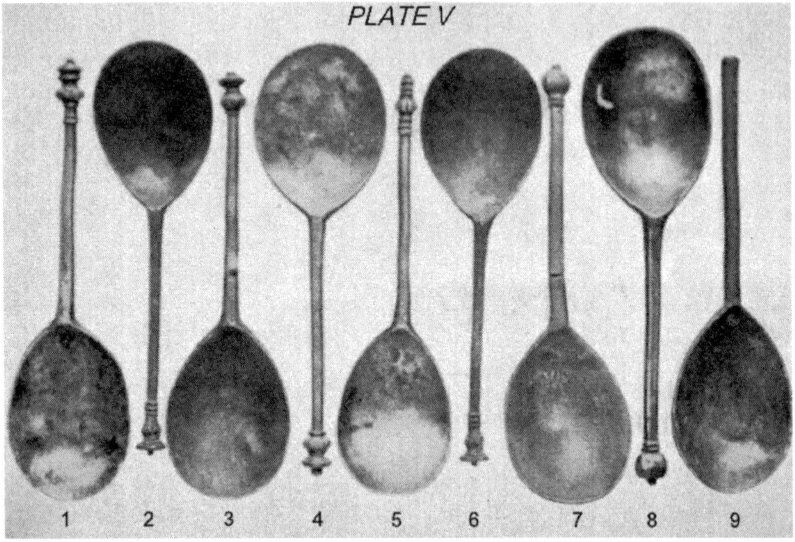

NOTES TO PLATE V

Approx. 40% actual size

16th century:

1. Baluster knop, mark:

2. Baluster knop, mark :

3. Baluster knop, mark :

4. Baluster knop, mark illegible

5. Baluster knop, mark:

Late 16th century

6. Baluster knop, mark:

7. Crown or Hexagonal knop, mark:

8. Crown or Hexagonal knop, mark :

9. Stump End, round stem, rat tail, mark :

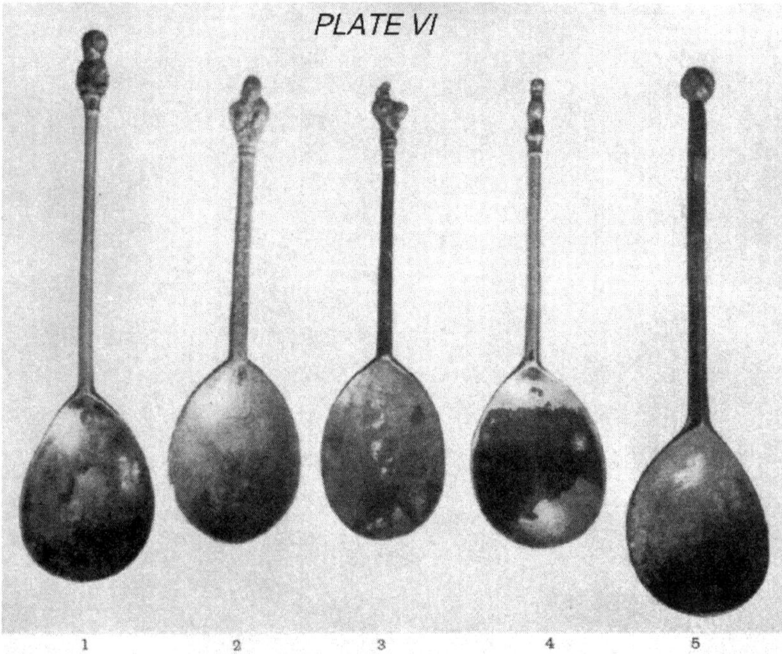

NOTES TO PLATE VI
Approx. 40% actual size

1. Monk's head: late 15th or early 16th century, mark:

2. Charles I head, or Maidenhead: 16th century, mark:

3. Chanticleer: end of 16th century, mark:

4. Sitting Lion: 16th century, mark:

5. Writhen, bronze, no mark: 14th-15th century.

SEAL TOPS

Pewter spoons of this type are uncommon and have the usual fig-shaped bowl, slender stems, with a sort of modified hexagonal section; frequently the upper and lower sides are flat, and in many cases the other sides are almost rounded off. Those with purely hexagonal stems are rare.

The stems terminate with a baluster knop, with a flat disc upon the top of it like a seal. These 'seals' on silver spoons are usually adorned with initials and dates, but those in pewter are usually plain. This type of spoon was in fashion from the middle of the 16th century to around 1660.

Marks found on pewter Seal Tops:

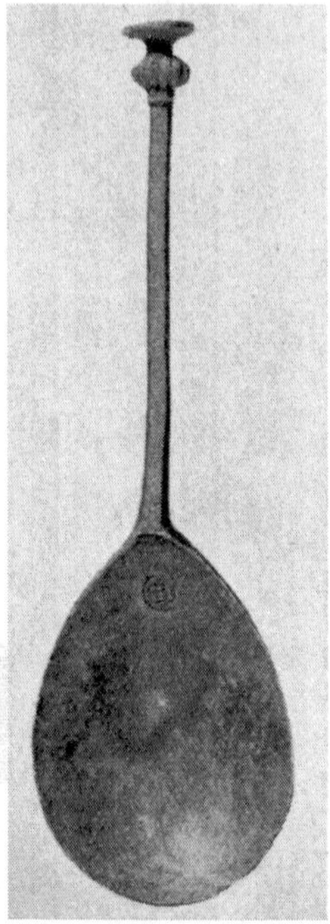

Fig. 21 Pewter Seal Topped Spoon Length: 6in/15.5cm

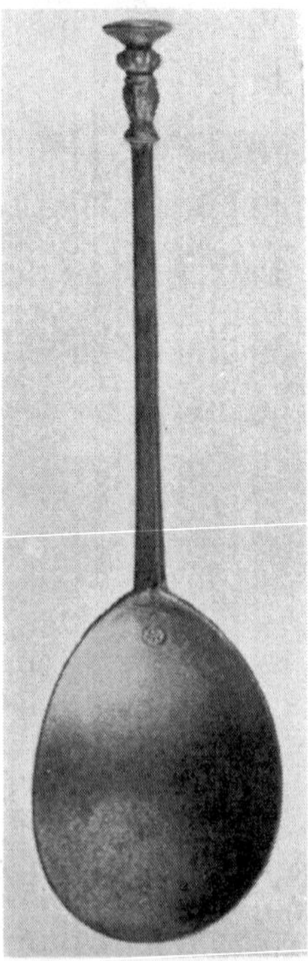

Fig. 22 latten Seal-Topped Spoon Length: 6.9in/17.4cm

Seal Tops were also made in latten and are much more numerous in that metal than they are in pewter. They had the same shape of bowl and the stems are four-sided. There were many makers of these spoons. The most usual stamps found in London are those bearing the marks of the rose or the fleur-de-lys in the bowl. Those marked with a rose are furnished with a baluster under the Seal Top; and those with the fleur-de-lys are much shorter in the stem, and end with a plain seal without a baluster. But there are many spoons with other marks on them. Those examples having the mark surrounded with a circle inscribed 'Double Whited' in the bowl were tinned and are dated to about 1670 or later. The other Seal Top latten spoons belong to the late 16th century and the first third of the 17th century. An early 17th century spoon bearing the fleur-de-lys mark, unusually has the owner's initial in the bowl:

G.
E. M.

Marks on Seal Top knops in latten:

STRAWBERRY KNOP

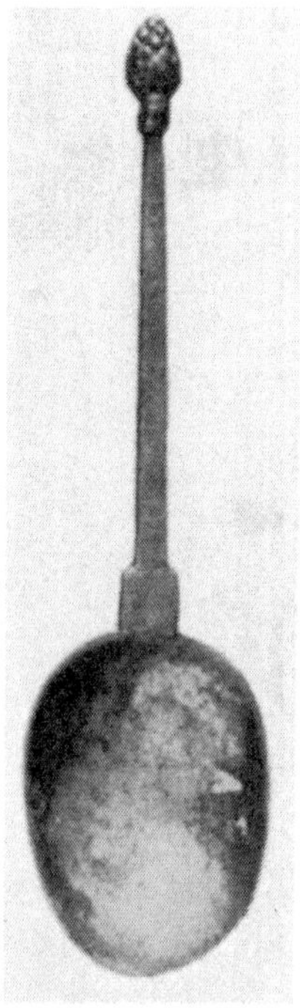

Fig. 23 Strawberry-Knopped Spoon Length: 6.4in/16.2cm

Spoons knopped with a fruit, such as a pineapple, appear to have been called commonly 'Strawberry Knops' and are of an early date and very rare in pewter. A poor example was found in Worship Street, dating to the 16th century; it has a fig-shaped bowl and hexagonal stem but is unmarked.

Silver 'de fradelett' spoons having this knop have been mentioned in a will in the year 1440 and an entry dated 1490 of six silver spoons refers to spoons knopped with a bunch of grapes or other fruit.

Examples are known in latten, such as that illustrated (*see* fig. 23), which has a flat stem and has been tinned.

Another has a small round bowl and both bear the mark of the same spoonmaker and date from about 1675; there is also a similar specimen in the British Museum.

Those made of brass, which have been found in London, with small fig-shaped bowls, dating to the 16th century, are most likely of foreign make. *See* Plate VIII.

Marks:

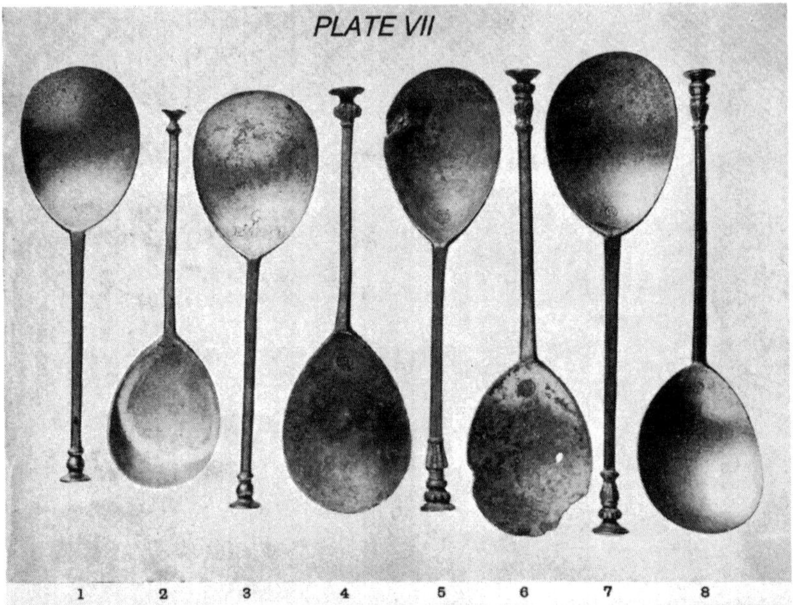

NOTES TO PLATE VII

Approx. 40% actual size

Late 16th or early 17th century:

1. Seal Top knop, latten, mark: 

2. Seal Top knop, latten: mark illegible.

3. Seal Top knop, latten, mark:  G
H M

4. Seal Top knop, pewter, mark: 

5. Seal Top knop, pewter, mark: 

6. Seal Top knop, latten, mark: 

7 & 8. Seal Top knop, latten, mark: 

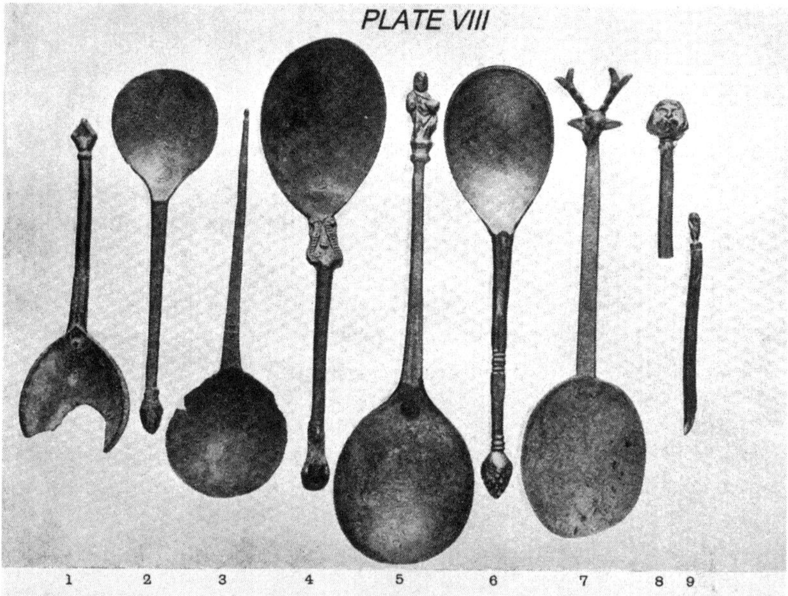

NOTES TO PLATE VIII

Approx. 40% actual size

1. Lozenge-shaped knop, flattened, round stem, ornamented on lower part of the stem and each side of the tongue behind; pewter. c.15th century. Mark:

2. Strawberry knop, latten: 17th century. Mark:

3. Latten round bowl, flat stem, decreasing in thickness towards the point, which is surmounted with a small round knop: c.14th century, probably French. Mark on stem:

4. Horsehoof knop, ornamental stem, pewter: 16th century. Mark:

5. Apostle, flat stem, latten tinned: early 17th century. Mark:

6. Strawberry knop, brass: 16th century. No mark.

7. Stag's head knop, latten, flat stem: 17th century. Mark: a rose?

8. Man's-head knop, latten. 16th century.

9. Writhen knop, stem only: the knop is gilt. 16th century.

SLIPPED IN THE STALKS

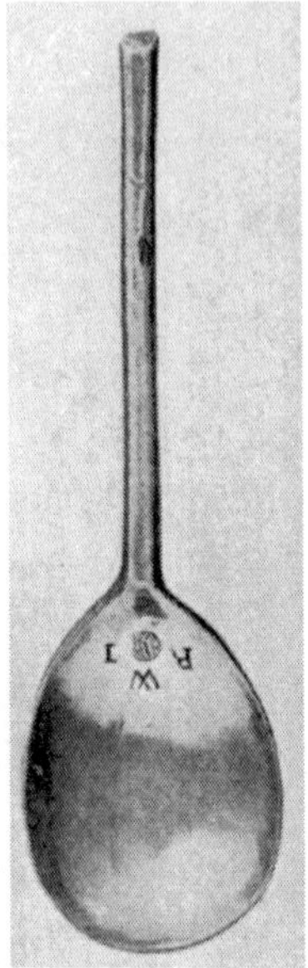

Fig. 24 Spoon Slipped in the Stalk
Length: 6.5in/16.4cm

This is a very simple type of spoon, in fact, the simplest of the whole series. These spoons have fig-shaped bowls and hexagonal or six-squared stems, with the ends cut off sloping up from the front of the spoon. The earliest forms had slender stems but towards the end of the 16th century and the beginning of the 17th century they were made generally stouter and stronger, occasionally supported with a short tongue on the back of the bowls.

They are frequently found with the initials of the owners stamped boldly in the bowls round about the touch, as in Fig. 24 and occasionally a single initial letter is cut upon the end of the stem.

Spoons of this type in silver are mentioned in the will of Thomas Rotherham, Archbishop of York, dated 1498 and described there as a dozen silver spoons 'Slipped in lez Stalkes.' It is reasonable to assume that pewter spoons of this type came into fashion early in the 16th century and continued in use with only slight modifications until the time of the Commonwealth (1649-60), during which time they are said to have been much used, probably because of their simplicity.

About the middle of the 17th century the form changed slightly, as the hexagonal stem had the upper and lower sides flattened and widened and the bowls became elliptical.

Latten spoons were also made but they are not so numerous as those made of pewter, probably because of the heavy penalties inflicted upon the pewter spoonmakers for making or selling spoons made of latten.

They remained in fashion throughout the reign of Charles II (1660-85) but had broad flat stems and were much like the 'Puritan' type.

An early spoon of 15th century type but which may be early 16th century, is marked in the bowl:  with the mark repeated, very unusually, three times.

Marks enclosed within a lozenge were probably used by female spoonmakers.

A spoon found in the crypt of Gloucester Cathedral Church and probably of local make is marked twice in the bowl with:

The following marks are very common on 'Slipped in the Stalk' spoons:

Marks on pewter 'Slipped in the Stalk' spoons:

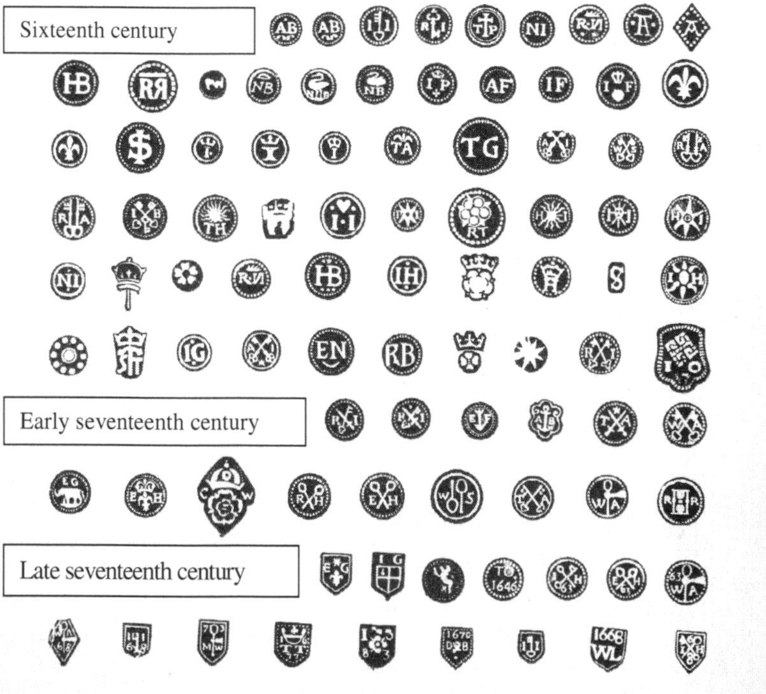

Marks on latten 'Slipped in the Stalk' spoons:

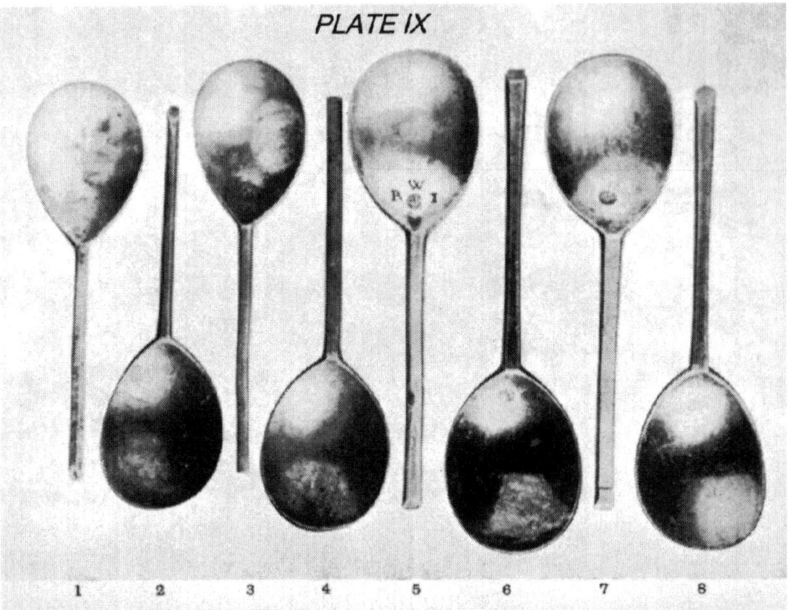

NOTES TO PLATE IX

Approx. 40% actual size

Late 16th – early 17th century:

1. Slipped in the Stalk, pewter: no mark.

2. Slipped in the Stalk, latten, mark:

3. Slipped in the Stalk, pewter, mark:

4. Slipped in the Stalk, pewter, mark:

5. Slipped in the Stalk, pewter, mark:

6. Slipped in the Stalk, latten, mark:

7. Slipped in the Stalk, pewter, mark:

8. Slipped in the Stalk, latten, mark:

PLATE X

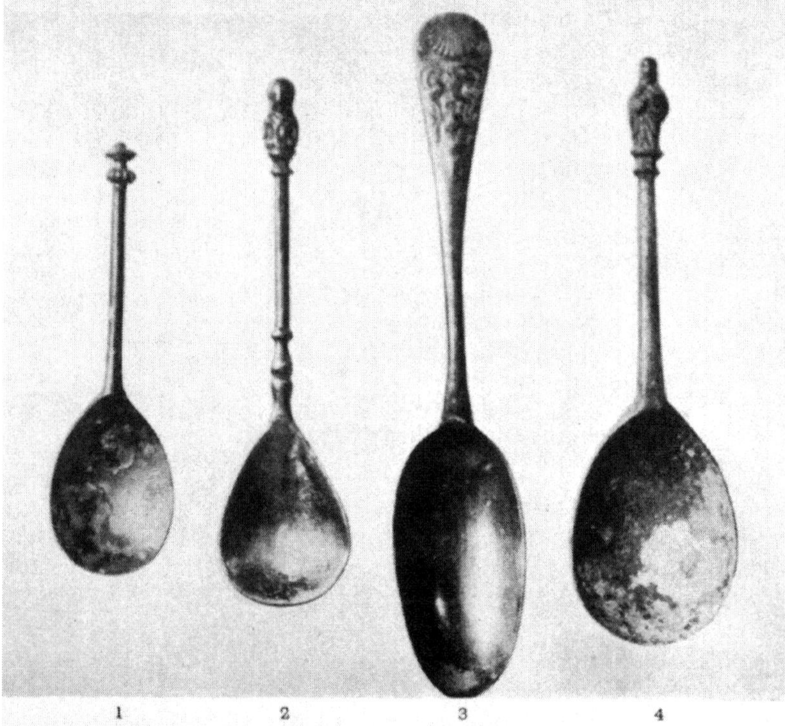

NOTES TO PLATE X

Approx. 40% actual size

1. Baluster knop, pewter, small size: early 16th century. Mark: 

2. Monk's head knop, brass; probably foreign: 16th century.

3. Rounded End, pewter: early 18th century.

4. Apostle, pewter: late 16th or early 17th century. Mark: 

PURITAN SPOONS

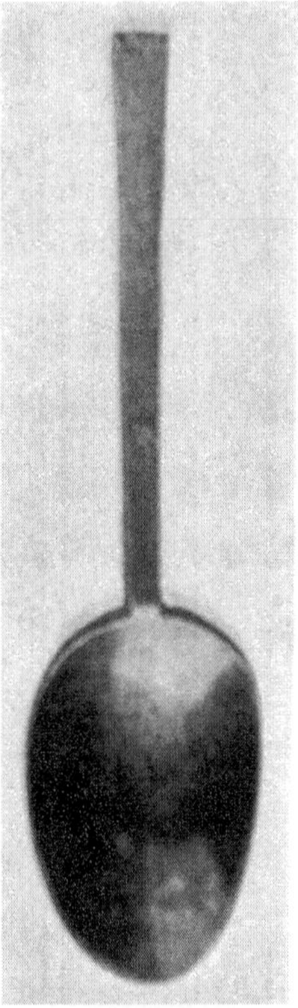

Fig 25 Puritan Spoon
Length: 6.3in/16cm

These came into fashion about the middle of the 17th century: a specimen is known in silver, bearing the date letter for 1651.

The bowls of these spoons change from the fig-shape, which had been in use for upwards of 200 years, into a large flat oval form and the width of the flat stalks or stems increases leaving the bowl to nearly double at the end, where two nicks are cut. This type has gradually developed from the 'Slipped in the Stalk' first by changing the shape of the stem from six-sided to four-sided, which became flatter and increased gradually in width to the cut-off end and, secondly, about 1660, by the bowl becoming a flat oval and the stem wider and flatter.

Puritan Spoons were made in pewter and latten and probably remained in use until after 1683, the latest date seen on a pewter spoon. A latten spoon marked with a rose on the back of the stem near the top, instead of in the bowl also indicates a later date.

Puritan spoons are frequently found with owners' initials boldly punched in the bowls. There are very few pewter spoons of this type that can really be separated from the flat stemmed 'Slipped in the Stalks.'

Marks on pewter spoons:

Marks on latten spoons:

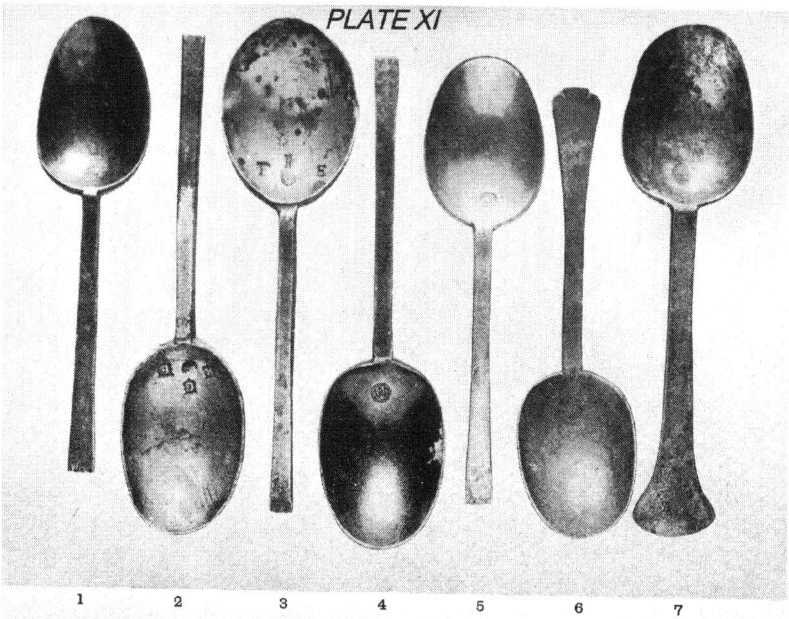

NOTES TO PLATE XI

Approx. 40% actual size

Mid 17th century

(All latten spoons have been tinned or 'double whited'):

1. Puritan, latten. Mark: 

2. Puritan, pewter. Mark: 

3. Puritan, pewter. Mark: 

4. Puritan, latten. Mark: 

5. Puritan, latten. Mark: 

6. Puritan, emerging into " Pied de Biche," latten. Mark: 

7. Puritan further development into "Pied de Biche," latten. Mark: 

PLATE XII

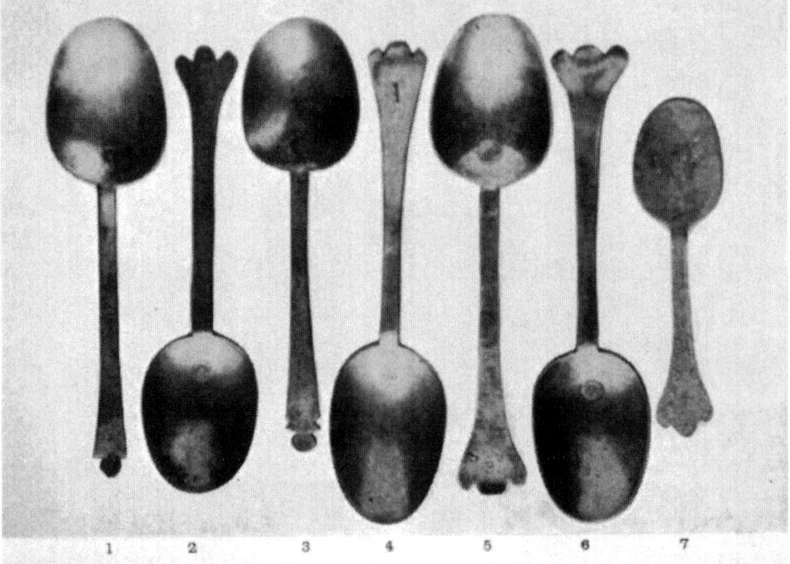

NOTES TO PLATE XII

Approx. 40% actual size

Last half of 17th century:

1. Split End, a variety, latten, tinned, mark:

2. Split End or Pied de Biche, latten, mark:

3. Split End, a variety, latten, mark:

4. Split End or Pied de Biche, latten, on end:  **mark:**

5. Split End, latten on handle; silvered, mark:

6. Split End, latten tinned, marked C on back, mark:

7. Split End, pewter, with heads of Charles II and his Queen on the handle, mark:

rest of mark worn away, probably C C.

'SPLIT ENDS' or 'PIED DE BICHE'

This type of spoon came into fashion about 1663. It was evolved out of the Puritan form (the bowls remaining the same shape), by simply hammering the end into a broad flat termination, into which two deep cuts were made. These spoons are supposed to have taken the name of 'Pied de Biche' from their similarity to a hind's foot. They are also sometimes called 'Trifids' or 'Trefids'.

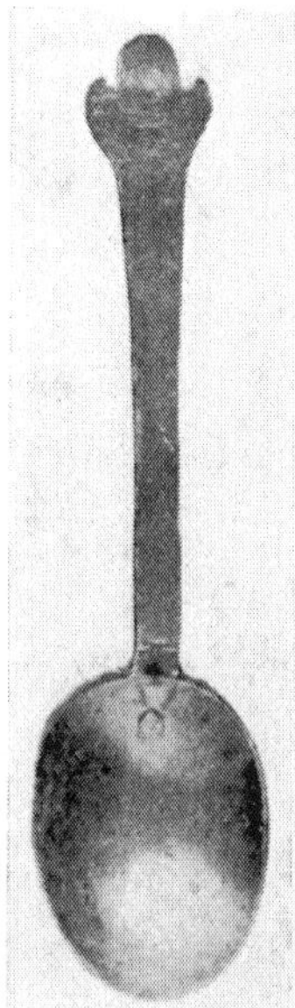

Fig. 26 Pewter Split-End or Pied de Biche Spoon Length: 6.9in/17.5cm

They are mostly strengthened on the backs of the bowls, with a tongue or rat-tail and a drop rather variable in form. The earliest are plain, while about 1670, these tongues are more accentuated by being hollowed on each side, and still later the stalks and backs of the bowls were ornamented with raised foliated work.

This spoon was made both in pewter and latten, and remained in fashion with variations in the termination of the stem, to the reign of George I (1715).

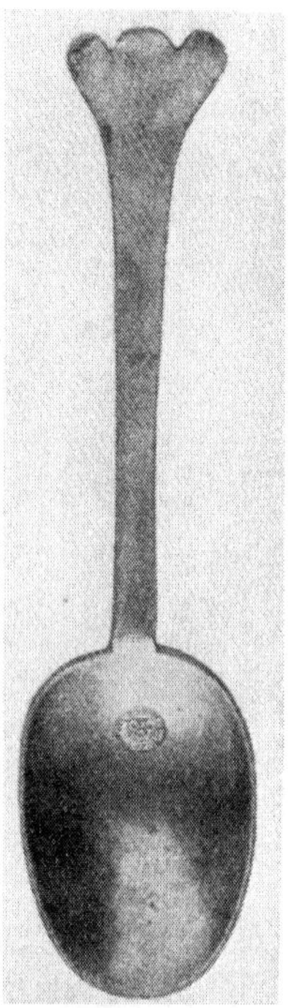

Fig. 27 Latten Split-End or Pied de Biche Spoon Length: 6.8in/17cm

After the middle of the 17th century, the makers of latten spoons were in the habit of tinning them, which gave them a silvery appearance, and they added to their marks a circle, round which they stamped 'Double Whited'.

In addition to the touch in the spoon bowl, which had remained up to about 1660 as the only mark, shortly after this date the pewterers punched two or three touches upon the back of the stem. Between 1680-1690 some of the spoonmakers left off placing their marks in the bowl and only marked them on the back of the stem with two or more touches, such as:

taken from a Split End spoon of this date. The earliest touch with a date is that of WL 1668, and it is also the earliest dated maker's mark in a shaped shield.

In a ledger of London Cutlers, Blanchard and Child for 1663, are many entries in the various accounts of 'French spoons' sold, and they are sometimes described as the 'New fashion spoon.' It may be assumed that these French spoons were the 'Pied de Biche,' as they undoubtedly first came into fashion about that date. It is also interesting to note that several

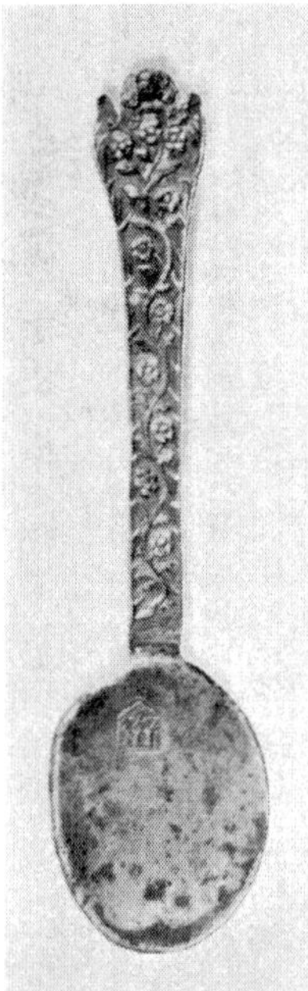

Fig. 28 Chocolate Spoon Length: 4in/10.2cm

people buying such ‘French spoons,’ paid for them by selling old spoons. Many spoons of this type bear the owner's initials stamped in the bowl.

There are many varieties in the end of the stem in the Pied de Biche spoons, as may be seen from examples in Plates XII-XIII. This type appears to have lent itself to the fancy of the spoonmakers, and many of the later spoons in addition to the touch in the bowl bear four marks on the back of the stem.

There is a small chocolate spoon of this type, which has a stem decorated with roses enclosed within a border of thorns up its entire length, terminating with a female bust between the clefts; the bowl is somewhat flattened. It is marked:

Another specimen of a chocolate spoon is shown on Plate XII; it also has a decorated stem, adorned at the end with the heads probably of Charles II and Queen Catherine, with a crown above them, and its length is 5 inches.

Marks on Split Ends in pewter:

Marks on Split Ends in latten:

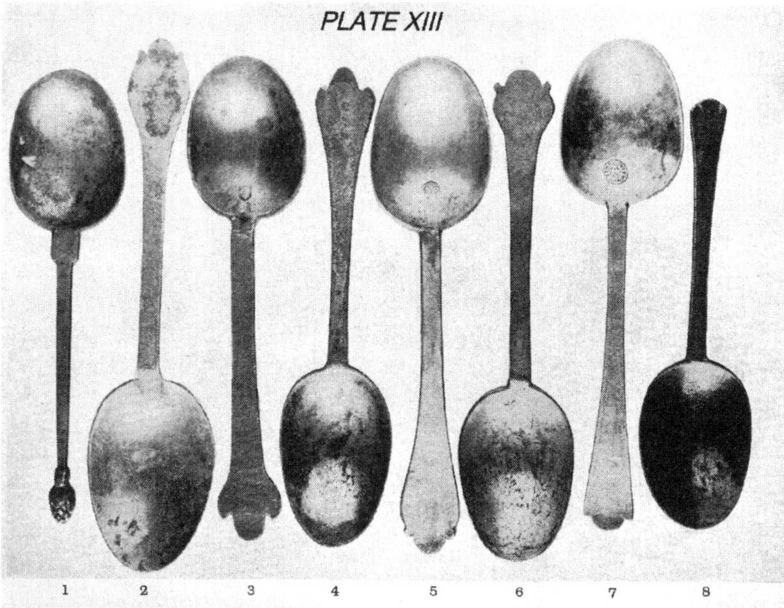

NOTES TO PLATE XIII
Approx. 40% actual size

Last half of 17th century:

1. Strawberry knop, latten tinned, mark:

2. Split End, pewter, rat tail: two stamps on stem. Mark:

3. Split End, pewter, rat tail, about 1680. Mark:

4. Split End, latten tinned: mark illegible.

5. Split End, a variety, latten tinned, mark:

6. Split End, a variety, latten tinned: mark illegible.

7. Split End, a variety, latten silvered: mark:
three illegible punch marks behind.

8. Puritan emerging into a Split End or Pied de Biche, latten, mark:

SHIELD END OR WAVY END SPOONS

This type came into fashion in the reign of William III (1694-1702). The change being that the end of the stem or stalk terminates with a wavy line, without the two clefts being cut into the top of the handle, as in the "Pied de Biche" type.

The stem is long and flat, but somewhat rounded at the bowl, which has a tongue or rat-tail on the back and is longer and narrower than earlier examples. Four marks are frequently found on the back of the stem, but none in the bowl. Spoons of this type are usually made of pewter and seldom of latten. There is a small-sized pewter spoon decorated along the stem, inside the bowl and upon the shoulders, dated to about 1700.

In some examples, the end is so much turned up towards the face that it almost forms a hook. Some specimens are known in silver, but in pewter the turned-over ends are invariably broken off.

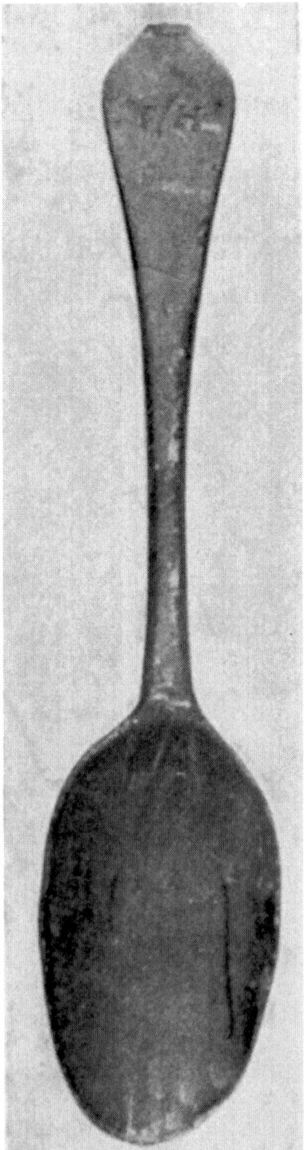

Fig. 29 Wavy Ended Spoon
Length: 7.25in/18.4cm

Shield or Wavy End marks:

ROUNDED ENDS

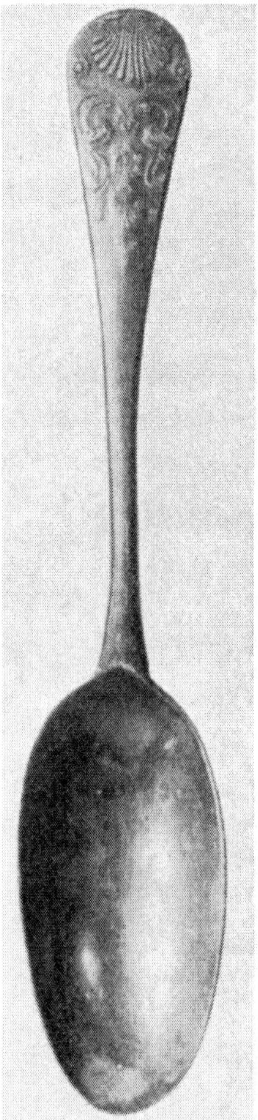

Fig. 30 Round Ended Spoon Length: 8in/20.4cm

The flatness which marked the upper half of the stem for about half-a-century is no longer seen. The wavy line at the extreme end with its projection in the centre has also disappeared, and for the first time, apparently, in the case of English spoons, the outline of the end is continued round from side to side in one unbroken curve. The end is still turned upwards towards the face, where a sharp ridge is formed, which is continued from the thick part at the extremity to about half way down the stem. It was furnished with a rat-tail on the back of the bowl.

Spoons of this type came into fashion in the reign of Queen Anne (1702-14) and continued towards the end of the reign of George II (1727-60) when the rat-tails gradually gave way, and a single or double drop took their place.

About 1767, the handle at the end of the stem was turned down instead of being turned up, as previously, and the bowl became longer, narrower and more pointed at the end. Spoons of this type had four touches upon the back of the stems.

An earlier type of the "Rounded End" spoon made of pewter, was in use many years before the type just described, somewhat similar to the "Puritan" spoons, but the ends instead of being cut off square and marked with three nicks, were rounded and somewhat turned up. The stems bear four or five marks on the backs, were flat and strengthened with a slight rat-tail on the back of the bowl. The spoonmaker's mark in the bowl was made in 1668:

Marks on Rounded Ends:

PLATE XIV

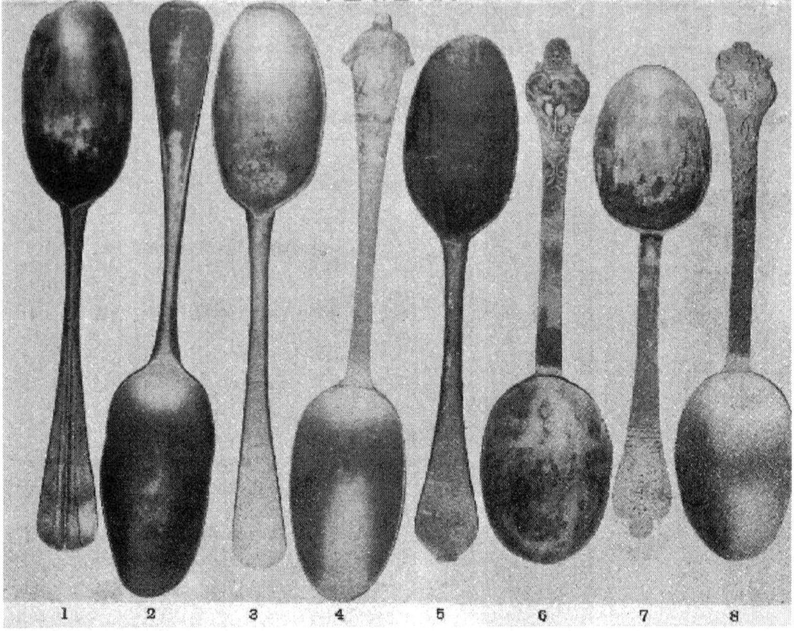

NOTES TO PLATE XIV **Approx. 40% actual size**

18th century:

1. Rounded End, pewter, with broad rib up front of stem, rat-tail,

marks: 

Crowned X. LONDON **Owner's initials:** I R I

2. Rounded End, pewter, long narrow bowl, long stem with end turning up, double drop at end of stem, terminating in a fan-like ornament, mark: VAUGHAN 

3. Rounded End, pewter, very similar, mark: R C

4. Wavy End with point, portraits of George III and Queen Charlotte, rat-tail, marks: 'Lamb and Flag', made in London, as no. 2,
I. VAUGHAN X **crowned.**

5. Wavy End, pewter, rat tail; LONDON; crowned X. I H.

Late 17th century:

6. Split End, pewter, decorated with foliage and scrolls, a crown between the ends, rat-tail, mark: 

7. Split End, pewter, rat, tail, crown decor on handle: no mark.

8. Split End (a variety) pewter, handle decorated with scrolls and M M, mark: 

PLATE XV

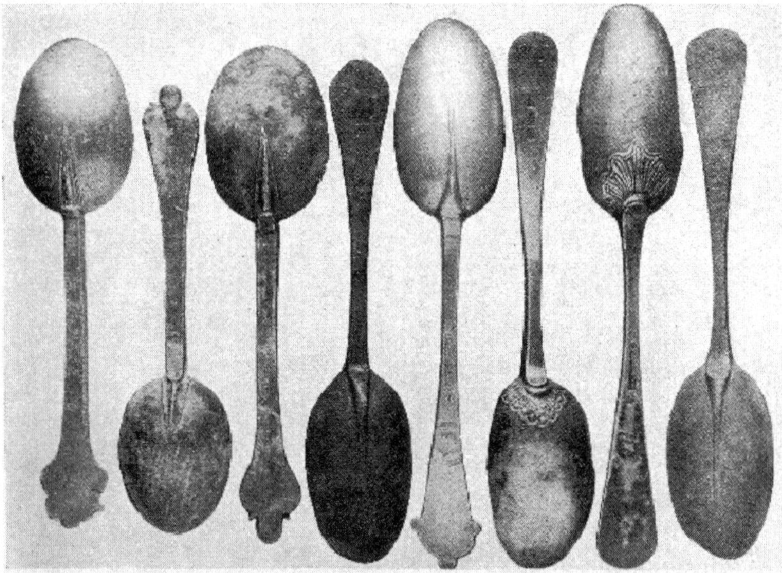

1 2 3 4 5 6 7 8

Back view of Spoons—Plate XIV.

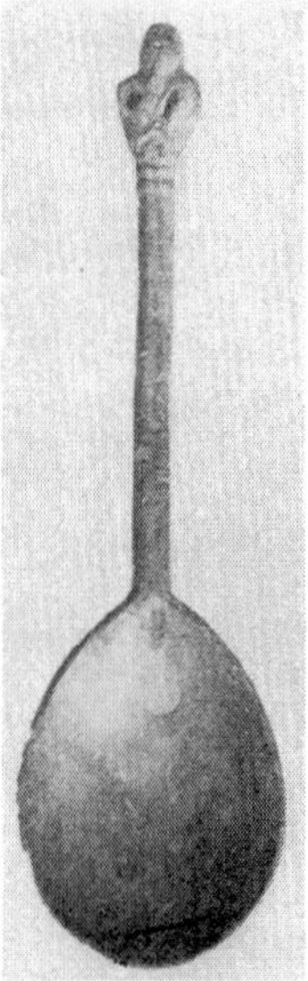

Fig. 31 Spoon with Maiden-head Knop Length: 6.25in/16cm

FANCY KNOPPED SPOONS

There are many other later types of pewter spoons that have been found in excavations in and about London, which will not be included here, as they are so like spoons in relatively modern use.

Plate XIV shows a few of the most interesting examples.

In addition to the types of spoons already described, there are others which are occasionally found which might be called Fancy-knopped spoons, of which only a few examples are known.

Fig. 31 is a small-sized pewter spoon of very coarse workmanship, having a flattened bowl somewhat fig-shaped and an hexagonal stem; it is well marked in the bowl with a crowned rose between the initials C and R. This might be easily mistaken for a royal badge, but it is probably only the mark or touch of the spoonmaker. The stem terminates in a knop not unlike the King's Head, but upon close examination it will be seen that the bust on the knop has large female breasts, so that it is probably only a

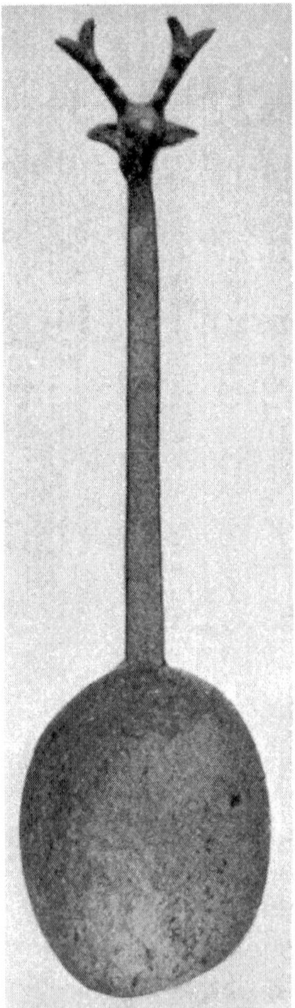

Fig. 32 Stag's Head Knop Spoon Length: 7in/18cm

debased form of a Maidenhead knop, which appears to date to the 16th century. Maker's mark:

STAG'S HEAD KNOP

This spoon has an elliptical bowl, with a flat stem tapering towards the end, which terminates in a well-defined stag's head and antlers as the knop. It is made of latten and was found in an excavation in the Tottenham Court Road. There has been a touch mark in the bowl, but unfortunately it is too worn to be decipherable. It probably dates about 1640.

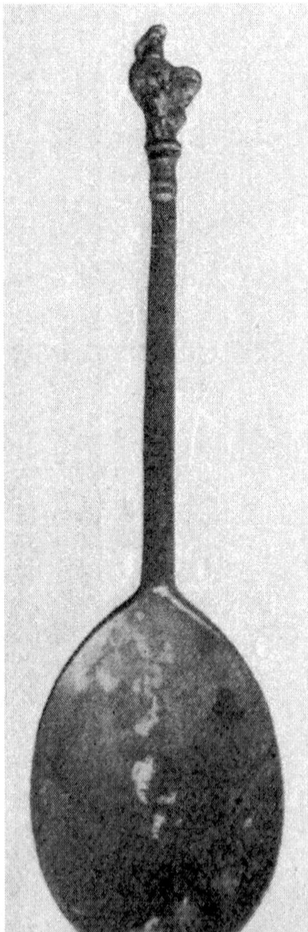

Fig. 33. Spoon with Cockerel Knop Length: 5.9in/15.5cm

COCKEREL KNOP

This is another very rare form of knop, the only one known is a small-sized spoon with an oval bowl, having a rounded stem terminating with a figure of a Cock. It is made of pewter and well marked on the bowl. It was found in London and probably dates to the late 16th century. Mark:

GLOBE KNOP

The bowl is of a rounded form, with a diamond section stem, having an ornamental cut near the bowl. At the end of the stem is a baluster, terminating with a geographical globe as a knop.

This spoon is made of latten, tinned over, and bears in the bowl the touch G.P. and three spoons:

this maker also made Seal Tops, Puritans, and Pied de Biches in Latten. Latter half of the 17th century.

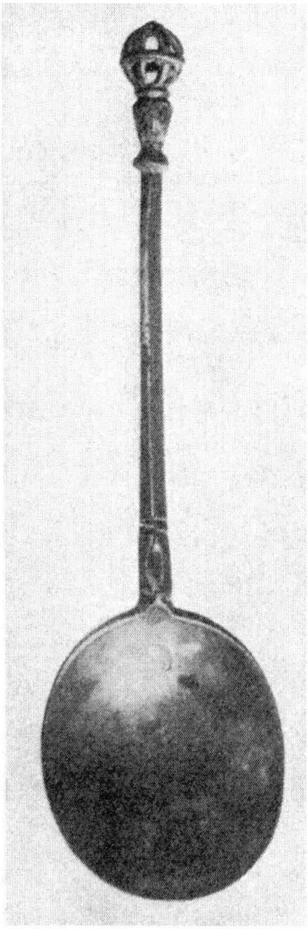

Fig. 34 Globe-knopped Spoon
Length: 6.9in/18cm

FLATTENED CONE KNOP

This is an unusual form of spoon, and has all the appearance of being of foreign make; but as it bears the mark of a spoonmaker who made Apostle spoons of precisely the same pattern and mark, it must be of English make, (fig. 35). It is of latten and has been tinned. The bowl is a semi-oval, broader at the base than it is at the stem, which is flat, with a central groove in it, terminating with a knop in the form of a flattened cone. Latter half of the 17th century. The mark is somewhat indistinct, but it bears portions of the words "DOUBLE WHITED."

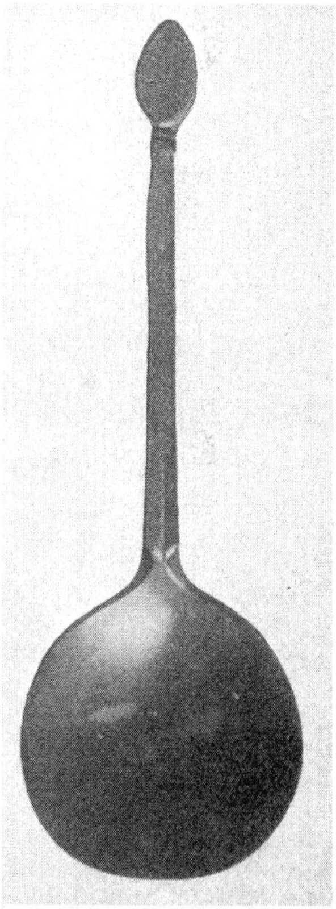

Fig. 35 Spoon with Flattened-cone Knop
Length: 6.8in/17.6cm

MAN'S-HEAD KNOP

This is a remarkable type of knop for a spoon and probably unique; all that remains of it is a short piece of the stem knopped with a man's head with long hair parted in the centre, heavy eyebrows and a large moustache (fig. 36).

The stem is hexagonal with a groove down the middle, similar to that in the latten Apostle spoons of the same period.

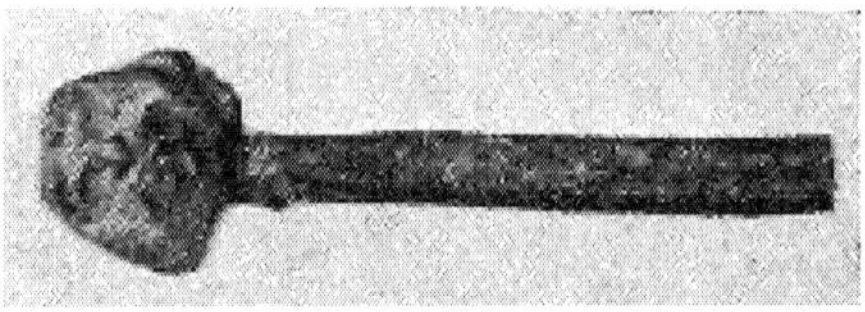

Fig. 36 Fragment of Man's-Head Knop Spoon
Length: 2.3in/6cm

It is made of latten and in the absence of the bowl and mark to identify it by, it is impossible to determine whether it is English or foreign make. It was found in the Thames at London, and probably dates to the latter end of the 17th century.

SMALL BRASS SPOONS

These spoons (fig. 37) have rather deep fig-shaped bowls; the stem is four-sided and plain for about 1.5 inch after leaving the bowl, it then takes a corkscrew twist, terminating in each case with a small cone-shaped knop. On the back of the bowl of one of the specimens, is engraved a church or gateway with a spire and small buildings on either side of it, upon the back of the other is a floral decoration. Both spoons were found in London but are probably of 15th century Russian or German make. They have no marks.

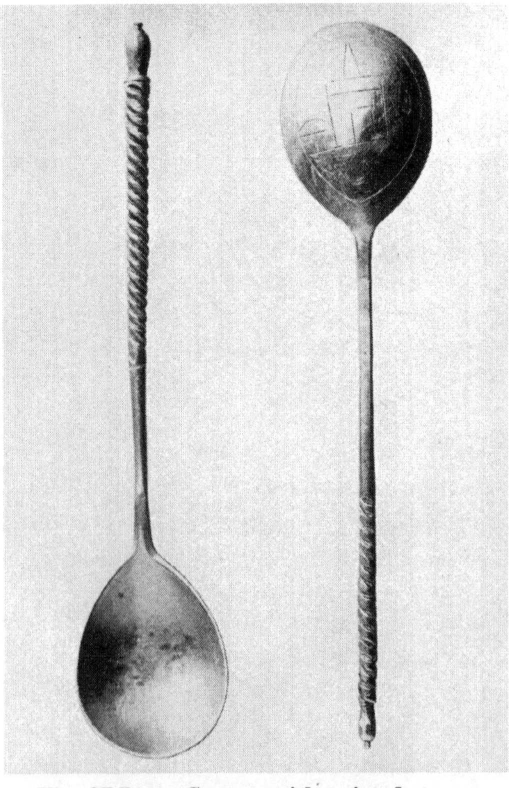

Fig. 37 Brass Spoons with twisted stems
Length: 5.4in/13.7cm

PASTRY CUTTER OR COOK'S SPOON

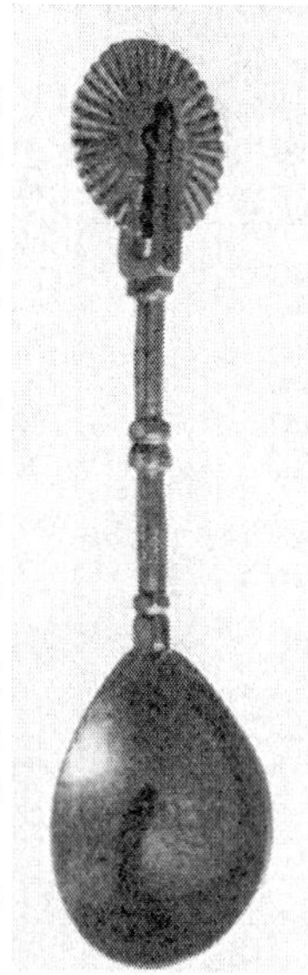

Fig. 38 Pastry Cutter or Cook's Spoon Length: 6in/15.2cm

This example (fig. 38) has a fig-shaped bowl with a round stem of baluster type, terminating with a moveable wheel, 1 inch in diameter, for cutting pastry.

It is made of latten, has no mark, and probably dates to the 17th century. It is not unusual to find similar spoons without the wheel attached.

There was an interesting custom of the Pewterers' Company in the fifteenth century, which obliged every new member to present a silver spoon to the Company upon his taking up the livery as shown by the following gift recorded 1487-8:

'Item 2 Spones of the gifte of Walt' Walshe and Kat'yne his Wiffe with his mark & name on the spoon and on the other Saynt-Kateryne giltid weiyng 2 ounces & half'

The above shows that Walshe gave two spoons to the Company bearing his mark, but the following extract from a later inventory of 1489-90 proves that the spoons were of silver, we can see from this that it was usual for the members to make silver spoons and punch their own touches on them: "Item. the gifte of Walter Walsh and Katryn his wyfe 2 silver sponys the toon gravyn on the ende his marke and gilte the tothyr spone havyng grave on the ende the ymage of seint katryn and gilte weyng 2 ounces & an halfe."

Many other similar entries of gifts occur in the records of the Company.

In 1504-5 "in the tyme of laurence Aslyn mr. Will'm pecok and Thomas outlawe wardeyns" the following order was passed by the Court:

"And it is ordeyned by the seid mr wardeyns and the hoole Compeigny of the seid crafte that from hensfurth every p'sone at his comyng in to the seid Clothyng shall bryng in and delyver unto the maister and wardeyns of the seid Crafte for the tyme beyng a silver spoone weiyng as above (i.e. an ounce and more) And this acte to endur unto the tyme that the halle shalbe stored of spones for as many p'sones as shalbe sett in the seid halle and parlour and after that to be converted to some other use necessarie and bihoffull."

In the years 1562 and 1590, the company sold a large number of spoons, and since that date they have gradually disposed of their stock.

Another instance of a pewterer's mark occurring on a late 16th century silver spoon of the Monk's-head type, has the mark in the bowl:

As silver spoons made by pewterers are very rare, fig. 39 illustrates two examples:

1. "Slipped in the Stalk" spoon bearing the touch, in the bowl, possibly of Daniel Barton:

2. "Pied de Biche or Split End" spoon with initials: I / W. E. on the back of the stem. It has a 'three-spoon' mark with the initial H. The other is obliterated.

Fig. 39 Silver Spoons bearing Pewterers' marks in the bowls

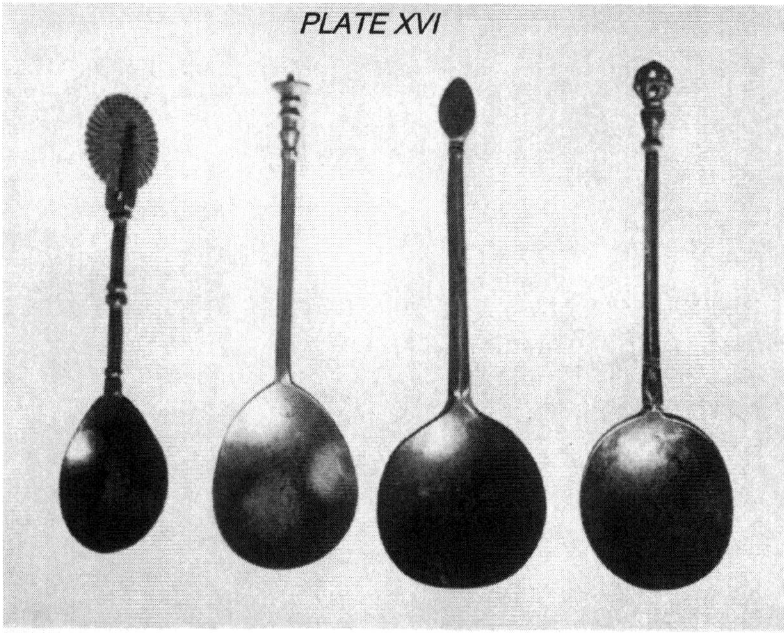

1 2 3 4

NOTES T0 PLATE XVI

Approx. 40% actual size

1. Pastry-cutter, latten; 17th century.

2. Baluster, latten: 16th century. Mark:

3. Flattened cone, latten; 17th century.

4. Globe, latten: late 17th century. Mark:

A careful examination of the marks on many hundred spoons has shown that a certain number of the marks are only found on the older types of spoons, such as those which were in fashion before the end of the 16th century.

The following analysis of these touch marks for each type of spoon relate to pewter spoonmakers of the 16th century or earlier but in the case of 'Slipped in the Stalks' spoons some of them may date to the first part of the 17th century.

Some of the forms of XVIth century pewter spoons or earlier, showing the different types known to have been made by each maker.	Acorns.	Maidenheads.	Writhens.	Lion Séjants.	Hexagonals.	Balusters.	Seal Tops.	Horsehoofs.	Slipped in the Stalks.	Stump End.	Apostle.
	*					*	*				
	*	*	*		*	*			*		
		*		*	*		*		*		
	*				*				*		
	*										
		*			*				*		
					*	*			*		

Some of the forms of XVIth century pewter spoons or earlier, showing the different types known to have been made by each maker.	Acorns.	Maidenheads.	Writhens.	Lion Séjants.	Hexagonals.	Balusters.	Seal Tops.	Horsehoofs.	Slipped in the Stalks.	Stump End.	Apostle
					*				*		
	*							*	*		
	*					*	*		*		
							*		*		
		*							*		
					*				*		
					*				*		
	*				*			*	*		
						*			*		
	*					*				*	*

The different touches of pewter spoonmakers using the same initials in the middle and latter part of the 17th century probably result from the order issued by the Court of the Pewterers' Company on 19th December, 1667: 'everie Spoon maker shall alter his touch imediatly after christmas next from w'ch tyme all Spoons shall be made exactly to ye Say.'

Thus the following variations of touches occur with the same initials:

FOUND ON:

Slipped in the Stalks.

Slipped in the Stalks.

Slipped in the Stalks.
Pied de Biche.

Slipped in the Stalks.

Slipped in the Stalks.
Pied de Biche.

Pied de Biche.

Slipped in the Stalks.

The following list of marks or touches taken from 17th century latten spoons shows a few examples of spoonmakers bearing the same initials using different touches. It is more likely that they were different individuals using the same initials than the same people having changed their marks as the pewter spoonmakers had to do after Christmas, 1667.

FOUND ON:

Apostle spoons (sometimes in a plain circle).

Seal Top spoon.

Slipped in the Stalk and Pied de Biche.

Pied de Biche.

FOUND ON:

Apostle spoons.

Pied de Biche.

Seal Tops, Puritans, Pied de Biche, and Globe.

Seal Tops, Puritans and Pied de Biche.

Seal Tops.

Pied de Biche.

Seal Top, Puritans, Slipped in the Stalks and Pied de Biche.

Slipped in the Stalks.

Pied de Biche.

Seal Top and Puritans.

Puritans.

SOME CONTINENTAL BASE METAL SPOONS

This chapter is not a comprehensive study of Continental base metal spoons generally, but seeks to illustrate and briefly describe a few spoons that differ from the ordinary types which were in general use in Britain and on the Continent.

With regard to the makers' marks, it is extremely interesting to find that as far back as the fourteenth century both pewter and latten were marked and in any period it is unusual to find pewter spoons, especially in Britain, unmarked but on the Continent comparatively few latten were marked, particularly in the seventeenth century.

Generally speaking, in Britain the pewter far outnumbered the latten. On the Continent it was the reverse. There is no doubt that a great many spoons, principally latten were imported into England from France and other countries. A peculiar flattened baluster knop from Belgium precisely matches a spoon in the British Museum which was found in London. Two specimens of latten beaded stems with hoof knops exactly alike, one from Northern Italy and the other found in London and a twisted stem spoon, with rough engraving of a church on the back, of which three at least have been found in London, are probably of Russian or German fifteenth century make. All these spoons are undoubtedly of foreign origin,

A curious feature about English base metal spoons is the absence of the round bowl. With the exception of a large soup spoon, with portraits of George III and Queen Charlotte, round bowl English pewter spoons are almost non-existent as are those in latten, brass or bronze, though a few latten are very nearly round, such as some of the apostle, the sitting lion knop and the globe knop. On the other hand, among Continental spoons we find the round bowl continually cropping up in pewter, latten and brass, in various sizes, from the fourteenth to the eighteenth centuries.

There is a considerable difficulty in dating many foreign spoons. In England the pewter and latten spoons, with few exceptions, were contemporary with or followed the silver spoons and the date letters of the latter settled the question but many Continental base metal spoons do not seem to have been made in silver. The recurrence of the round bowl and the absence of the makers' marks add to the difficulty in many cases.

Approx. 40% actual size

1. Pewter; found in the river Scheldt at Antwerp. A fine example of twisted stem (rare in pewter), with the badge of Flanders-a lion and a shield-as a knop. Sixteenth century. Mark: crown, hammer, and initials indistinct.
2. Pewter (Flanders). This is an uncommon type, and difficult to date, but, its extreme lightness (just over ¾oz./21gm.) points to its being an early spoon, probably fourteenth or fifteenth century.
3. Pewter (Dutch). A form of Maidenhead knop with a decorated stem. The knop is certainly not beautiful, and is very different from some of the English Maidenhead spoons. Sixteenth century.
4. Brass; country of origin unknown. This is an early spoon with a kind of finial knop; probably fourteenth or fifteenth century.
5. Latten, probably French. Another type of Maidenhead. Seventeenth century.

Approx. 50% actual size

6. Pewter (Dutch). A fine example of the hoof knop. This form of knop seems to have been much commoner in Holland than in England, where they are very rare in pewter. Seventeenth century. Mark: crown over rose.
7. Pewter (Dutch). A pretty round bowl spoon with tulip knop. Sixteenth or seventeenth century. Mark: crown over hammer.
8. Pewter (Dutch). An interesting example of the Trifid or pied de biche" spoon with portrait of William of Orange, afterwards King William the Third of England. About 1685. Hall-marks, all in shields: (1) Initials, possibly J. F. and two stars. (2) Buckle and two stars. (3) Lion rampant and two stars.
9. Latten (Northern Italy). Note the peculiar flat rectangular top, evidently for some special purpose. A smaller spoon with similar knop is known, but much cruder and earlier. Date, seventeenth century.

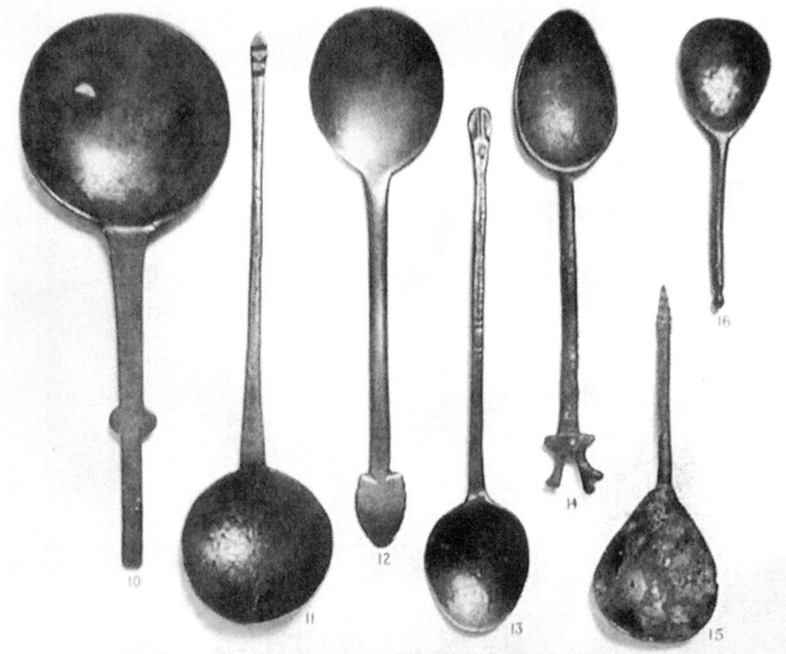

Approx. 50% actual size

10. Latten (Antwerp). A very heavy spoon of unusual shape. Probably seventeenth century.

The next three or four spoons are of the peculiar small shallow bowl type, for which it is difficult to assign a use. They are of different periods and seem to have had no counterpart in England.

11. Latten ; found in the river Scheldt at Antwerp. Shallow bowl and flat stem. Probably fifteenth century.

12. Latten (Belgium). Very shallow bowl and flat handle with strawberry knop. Probably sixteenth century.

13. Latten (Northern Italy). Shallow bowl with bended stem and horsehoof knop. Seventeenth century. Mark: star and (illegible) in beaded oval.

14. Latten; said to have been found in England but probably Continental. Knop similar in outline (only) to the stag's head. The bowl is raised above the stem. Date uncertain. Most likely seventeenth century.

15. Pewter (Belgium). A small spoon with baluster knop. Probably a child's or toy spoon, as salt-spoons were not used before the eighteenth century. The date is sixteenth century. Mark: crown over rose.

16. Latten cone end. Probably Continental. Fourteenth or fifteenth century.

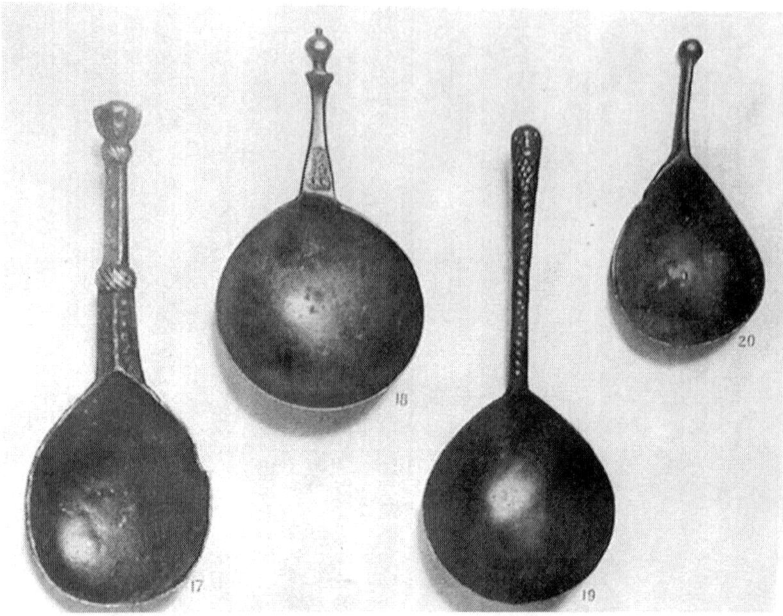

Approx. 50% actual size

17. Pewter (Dutch). Cherub's head knop with inscription, 'Drinck und is got nicht vergis' (Low German) — 'Drink and forget not God.' Use and date uncertain.
18. Latten (German). An apothecary spoon, fifteenth or sixteenth century. Note the fine merchant's (not maker's) mark. These marks were used in Germany from the fourteenth to the sixteenth century.
19. Latten (French). Wild-man knop with decorated stem, which is flat at the back. Possibly an apothecary's spoon, but more likely a domestic one. Probably seventeenth century. Mark: fleur-de-lys crowned in shield.
20. Latten (Northern Italy). Ball knop. Undoubtedly an apothecary's spoon of the fifteenth century.

The extremely interesting latten spoon illustrated right, approximately 40% actual size, was found in the Thames but is probably Continental. Several experts consider it unique and, while agreeing that it is not early Christian, nearly all date it before the cone ends of the fourteenth century. If this verdict is correct, it means that it is the earliest type of medieval spoon known and may be thirteenth century or considerably earlier.

In conclusion, the Continental spoons illustrated here are difficult to date and do not represent the ordinary types but rather the odds and ends that are found from time to time.

BIBLIOGRAPHY

Bailey, Gordon, *Detector Finds 2,* (Greenlight Publishing, 1993)

Hilton Price, F G, *Old Base Metal Spoons with Illustrations and Marks,* (London, 1908)

Jackson, C J, *An Illustrated History of English Plate,* (London, 1911; New York, 1967); 'The Spoon and its history; its form, material and development, more particularly in England', in *Archaeologia,* vol. LIII, (1893)

Massé, T. L. J., *Pewter Plate. A Historical and Descriptive Handbook* (London, 1904)

Port, Chas G J, 'Some Continental Base Metal Spoons', in *The Connoisseur,* vol. XXXIII, May-August, (1912)

Villanueva, David, *Metal Detecting, Genealogy and Family History:How to Find Heirlooms and Ancestors Through the Metalwork They Left Behind,* (True Treasure Books, 2006)

Welch, C., *History of the Worshipful Company of Pewterers of the City of London* (London, 1902),

GREAT BOOKS IN PRINT BY THE SAME AUTHOR

THE SUCCESSFUL TREASURE HUNTER'S SECRET MANUAL: Discovering Treasure Auras in the Digital Age, Soft Cover, 210mm x 146mm, 68 pages, (True Treasure Books, 2009) ISBN 978 0 9550325 5 4

CLEANING COINS & ARTEFACTS: Conservation * Restoration * Presentation, Soft Cover, 210mm x 146mm, 110 pages, (Greenlight Publishing, 2008) ISBN 978 1 897738 337

PERMISSION IMPOSSIBLE: Metal Detecting Search Permission Made Easy, Soft Cover, 210mm x 146mm, 52 pages, (True Treasure Books, 2007) ISBN 978 0 9550325 3 0

SITE RESEARCH FOR DETECTORISTS, FIELDWALKERS & ARCHAEOLOGISTS, Soft Cover, 250mm x 190mm, 160 pages, (Greenlight Publishing, 2006) ISBN 1 897738 285

SUCCESSFUL DETECTING SITES: Locate 1000s of Superb Sites and Make More Finds, Soft Cover, 250mm x 190mm, 238 pages, (Greenlight Publishing, 2007) ISBN 978 1 897738 306

THE ESSENTIAL GUIDE TO OLD, ANTIQUE AND ANCIENT METAL SPOONS, Soft Cover, 210mm x 146mm, 88 pages, (True Treasure Books, 2008) ISBN 978 0 9550325 4 7

THE SUCCESSFUL TREASURE HUNTER'S ESSENTIAL DOWSING MANUAL: How to Easily Develop Your Latent Skills to Find Treasure in Abundance, Soft Cover, 210mm x 146mm, 60 pages, (True Treasure Books, 2005) ISBN 0 9550325 0 4

MY ANCESTOR LEFT AN HEIRLOOM: Discovering Heirlooms and Ancestors Through the Metalwork They Left Behind, Soft Cover, 210mm x 146mm, 84 pages, (True Treasure Books, 2011) ISBN 978 0 9550325 6 1 (Replaces **METAL DETECTING, GENEALOGY and FAMILY HISTORY**)